600

MW01038725

MY ANALYSIS
WITH FREUD

Reminiscences

OTHER BOOKS BY A. KARDINER, M.D.

The Individual and His Society
Traumatic Neuroses of War
The Psychological Frontiers of Society
The Mark of Oppression, with Lionel Ovesey
Sex and Morality
They Studied Man, with Edward Preble

Dr. A. Kardiner zur freundlichen Erinnerung an seinen Aufenthalt in Wien 1921/22 Sigm. Freud 30.3.22

MY ANALYSIS
WITH FREUD
Reminiscences

A. KARDINER, M.D.

W · W · NORTON & COMPANY · INC ·
NEW YORK

Copyright © 1977 by A. Kardiner. All rights reserved. Published simultaneously in Canada by George J. McLeod Limited, Toronto. Printed in the United States of America.

First Edition

Library of Congress Cataloging in Publication Data
Kardiner, Abram, 1891–
    My analysis with Freud.
    1. Psychoanalysis—Biography. 2. Kardiner, Abram,
1891–   3. Freud, Sigmund, 1856–1939. I. Title.
RC506.K37   616.8'917'0924 [B]   76-55343

ISBN 0-393-01135-6

1 2 3 4 5 6 7 8 9 0

To my stepmother, Rachel Mayer,
and
my wife, Ethel Diana

Contents

Foreword

THERE ARE very few people today who have had the privilege of a personal analysis by Freud himself. By a series of accidents, I came to his attention by way of H. W. Frink. At a younger age, I would hesitate to reveal biographical material necessary for such a venture. At my age, however, what matters most is not a contribution to Freudiana, about which abundant material is already in existence. My motive is a bit different—to reveal his technique, insofar as it is possible, in a single case done by Freud.

At the time I was in Vienna, 1921–1922, he had nine patients and, so far as I can tell, he did not treat them all alike. Most of those who were there at the time complained that he never said anything. Some left disappointed and some felt they got nothing from the experience.

I got a great deal out of it. When I saw him again in 1927, in his summer home in Semmering, he looked ill, he had lost much weight, but he did remember that we had both had an exciting time of it. And I still look upon it as one of the peak experiences of my life. This is what makes up the content of this book—Freud the analyst and Freud the man, and the scientific obligations under which this experience put me. Of the latter, I can only say that I followed my scientific conscience—rightly or wrongly.

This small volume concerns itself chiefly with my own analysis and forms part of a larger biography dictated to Bluma Swerdloff, collected by her for the Columbia University Living Biography series.

A special thanks to Herbert Hendin and Josephine Hendin for their valuable help in preparing this manuscript for publication. I am indebted to my wife and collaborator, to whom I have, in part, dedicated this work.

A. K.

New York, 1976

1

Meeting with Freud

April 10th 21

WIEN, IX . BERGGASSE 19.

Dear Dr Kardiner

I am glad to accept you
for analysis especially
as Dr Frink has given
so good an account of you.
He is strongly confident of
your chances as an analyst
and speaks highly of your
character.

Six months are a good term
to achieve something both
theoretically and personally.
You are requested to be
at Vienna on the first
of October as my hours
will be given away
shortly after my return
from the vacation, and
give me definite assurance
of your coming some
time before — Let us say
in the beginning of
Sept.

My fees are $10 an hour
or about $250 monthly. to be
paid in effective notes
not in checks, which I could
only change for Kronen.

If you understand and
talk German it will
be a great help to our
analysis and you can work
here in the Redaktion
of the Internat. Ps. a.
Press

With kind regards
yours truly
Freud

L ATE IN APRIL 1921, I received a letter from Freud which read as follows:

Dear Dr. Kardiner,

I am glad to accept you for analysis especially since Dr. Frink has given so good an account of you. He is strongly confident of your chances as an analyst, and spoke highly of your character.

Six months are a good term to achieve something both theoretically and personally. You are requested to be in Vienna on the first of October, as my hours will be given away shortly after my return from the vacation, and give me definite assurance of coming some time before—let us say, in the beginning of September.

My fees are $10.00 an hour or about $250 monthly to be paid in effective notes, not in checks which I could only change for crowns.

If you understand German, it would be a great help to our analysis, and you can work here in the Redaktion of the Intern. Jour. of Psa.

With kind regards,

> *Yours truly,*
> FREUD

This letter changed my fate and my world. To be an apprentice to one of the great figures of our time! I had been in psychoanalytic practice for a little over a year and was also medical examiner at the Children's Court. At the time, there were all of eight practicing psychoanalysts in New York.

I knew that I was in a new and exciting field of medicine and felt that the training I had received up to now was inadequate to the task it purported to do. And now I would have the opportunity to study with the man who discovered and opened up this door to the mysteries of the human mind. I had written to Freud at the urging of my training analyst, Dr. Horace W. Frink, but felt some trepidation. After all, this was a world-renowned figure and I could think of no good reason for his favoring me. But here was a positive reply in my hand!

I had four months to wait; to go first to Paris and then by Orient Express to Vienna. I was looking forward to seeing Europe, especially Paris. I scraped together $2,200 ($500 of which my father gave me, the rest I saved from my earnings). The trip was through the Swiss Alps, and we finally arrived in Vienna. Monroe Meyer, who had been there for six months with a severe neurosis, was my guide. He found me a place to live in an apartment on one of the great squares of Vienna (24 Schottenplatz), which I had to vacate after a sojourn of two days, because the bedbugs prevented me from sleeping.

Monroe Meyer recommended that we go to meet Freud at the railroad station. I was disappointed. I expected a taller man, and he had a raucous, cracked voice; but he spoke impeccable English. Freud extended his hand, introducing me to his wife, his daughter Anna, and to Paula, the girl who opened the door to Freud's professional end of the apartment. We were advised to be at his office the following day, Monday.

Although we had exchanged only a few words, I had an immediate, implicit trust in Freud. He had an air of authority and strength and I felt completely at ease with him and myself. I was certain that this man could not only help me personally, but would launch me on a most exciting career.

In my preliminary interview with Freud, he asked for a biographical sketch, which I did in a condensed form. At one point, he interrupted with a question, "And what did you get out of your analysis with Dr. Frink?" to which I replied, "Nothing," and went on with my story. At the end of forty minutes, he said, "I think you are a very interesting personality to work with, but you made one statement which I would like to correct. You said you got nothing out of your analysis with Frink. You are wrong. You did get something out of it." "What did I get?" To which Freud replied laconically, "A little neurosis."

"And now," he proceeded, "I must raise a difficult question. You are five Americans (Polon, Blumgart, Oberndorf, Meyer, and you) and a Swiss gentleman. I had normally expected, under conditions like this, that at least one of you would drop out. I know that you have all changed lives in order to come here, but I have only thirty hours for all of you. Would any of you wish to go to Karl Abraham in Berlin, Otto Rank, or Sandor Ferenczi in Budapest? All of them are great at their craft. Would you?"

"No!" I said.

"Well, we shall see. I shall discuss it with my wife and daughter, Anna. I am willing to take on an extra hour of work, but they won't hear of it. In any case, I will see all of you tomorrow at three, and we will reach some conclusion."

At which, as was customary from that time on, he extended his hand and drew me slightly to him, saying, *"Auf Wiedersehn!"*

This allotment of time and the possible dropping of one of us was a serious situation, because at the time Freud was the only training analyst to whom foreigners would go.

We all gathered the next day at 3 P.M. and were ushered into his office. "Well, gentlemen, my daughter, my wife, and I have reached a conclusion, which I hope will suit all of you. My daughter Anna made the best suggestion. Being something of a mathematician, she figured out that $6 \times 5 = 30$, and $5 \times 6 = 30$. So if each of you will sacrifice one hour per week, I can accommodate all of you." We all agreed, and that was the beginning of the five-hour week. Heretofore, it had been six hours weekly. Tradition yielded to expediency. Yet this expediency in its turn became a tradition. Interestingly enough, James Strachey, Alix Strachey, and John Rickman, the English contingent, did not have to sacrifice one hour a week. We mere Americans could be sacrificed.

My hours were staggered: Monday at three, Tuesday at four, Thursday at six, Friday at three, and Saturday at six. As one entered the apartment, one stepped into a foyer, to the right of which was a clothes hanger. The furniture in the waiting room was Victorian—red plush sofa, a small round table, and two chairs. On the round table were a lamp and a family album which I perused many times, though I could not identify any of the characters.

Since there was a five-minute pause between patients, and everybody came early, people rarely met in the foyer. To usher the patient into the office, Freud opened the door to the waiting room, with an extended hand coming and leaving. One walked forward and into the main study. There was one large window in the room facing the courtyard, in which stood a large chestnut tree. The sofa was against the left wall in those days, and was subsequently moved to the center wall. In back of the sofa was Freud's chair, and in front of it a brass spittoon. The wall at right angles to the sofa and also facing the courtyard was a large sectional bookcase, to which he occasionally went to verify a reference. Thus, on one occasion, he got up to show me Goethe's poem "The Sorcerer's Apprentice" ("Der Zauberlehrling"). Some fifteen feet to the left of the sofa were two abutments, leading to Freud's famous writing desk, on which were many Egyptian statuettes. In the left abutment was a porcelain stove. The writing desk looked out on a small balcony and overlooked the chestnut tree and garden. The entire apartment was on the mezzanine floor. The staircase on the right led to Freud's professional corner; the left staircase led to the living quarters. On the left staircase I often saw Mrs. Freud, Martha, usually with a wicker basket filled with food packages.

2

My Analysis

I WENT TO my first hour with complete confidence in Freud, no apprehension, and I felt certain that he could solve the problem that my analysis with Frink had brought about. Needless to add, I was quite certain that I could learn much from the adventure on which I was embarked.

Freud ushered me into the study, pointed to the sofa, and said, "You know what to do!" And so I began.

I am thirty years old. My father was a tailor who came to America in 1884, when he was twenty-eight years old. He had lived in a *shtetl* in the deep Ukraine, somewhere in the neighborhood of Vitebsk, Zhitomir, and Berdichev, in the province of Vladimir. He often told the story of how he fled from the persecutions in Russia, and because he could not make a living. My father was the oldest of three boys, and in accordance with the Russian law was exempt from military duty. But since the younger two had disqualified themselves by some form of self-mutilation, my father did get into the army, and was assigned to the band, where he was taught to play the trumpet. From the many stories he told, I gathered that he was quite popular with women. In any case, he served four years, from age nineteen to twenty-three.

Apparently, my father was his mother's favorite, and

she feared that once out of the army, he would leave the village for America. To forestall this move, she picked out a girl and prevailed upon my father to marry her. She was Mildred Wolfe. This, she thought, would keep him in Russia. Before he went into the army at age nineteen, my father apprenticed himself to the village tailor.

There were several other apprentices and a peasant who served as handyman. The other boys urged my father to ask this peasant to tell his fortune. This peasant was either very good at his craft or a good guesser. Warning my father not to look into the future, he finally surrendered. He told my father of a troubled future. I still remember every detail. "You will be a soldier. The money your family has lent to a nearby 'nobleman' will never be paid back. [This would be the entire family savings.] You will be very ill. You will marry. You will have seven children. Your wife will die. You will remarry. Your second wife will have no children. You will live to an old age and die a relatively wealthy man."

My father was apparently dazed by this prophecy. But all of it came true. He did become a soldier, he did marry, reluctantly, I think. After his marriage, he had a daughter, my sister (eight years my senior). He had typhus. He could no longer make a livelihood in his own village. He decided therefore to migrate to America. Since there were no passports in those days, moving to America was managed by a kind of band of gangsters who collected fees for the local police, the border guards, the railroad, and the ship companies. It took a lot of skimping to gather the money to effect transportation to the United States. Some got there, some did not, and some landed in jail.

My father sailed from Liverpool (then the great emigration port of exit for European emigrants) on a ship called *Columbia*, and landed at Ellis Island in New York in 1884. His intention was to get a job, save, and send for my mother and sister.

There was a depression during the Cleveland administration and he could not make a living. He moved about from one place to another. Somehow he conveyed to me the idea that some places were "lucky" and others were "unfortunate." However, he finally settled in Philadelphia and earned enough money as a tailor to send for my mother and sister, who was five or six years old. Shortly after their arrival, they moved to New York, where I was born on August 17, 1891.

My mother had to go to the East River with a bucket and carry a heavy pail of coal, distributed by some charity or other, and carry it home over a long distance. In the meanwhile, I was a neglected child, living under conditions close to starvation.

I have a few memories of those dark ages; one of being very small and playing on the floor with another little boy. An angry woman slapped my hand and went back to sit on a chair at a table—the only furniture in the room. Another memory was being put out on a fire escape to see during some festive occasion. Bands were playing and flags waving. I was then about fourteen months old, and the occasion must have been Columbus Day, the four-hundredth anniversary of the discovery of America.

On one of my mother's trips to the East River, she caught a cold, which persisted, and was finally diagnosed as pulmonary tuberculosis, from which she died in 1894, when I was three years old. Tuberculosis in those days was supposed to be hereditary, and "scrofula," as it was commonly called, was something to be ashamed of. All I remember of the period related to my mother's death was being taken from one house to another by one of my uncles. He walked rapidly, and I had to run to keep up with him. He took me into a house filled with weeping people. My father lifted me in his arms as he stood over a pine box in which my shrouded mother lay. Then there was a funeral, the corpse being carried by two men on a kind of stretcher. Prayers in an unknown language were chanted. I later found out the prayers were in Hebrew. That evening no one was at home. A dark room lit by a kerosene lamp. Someone was playing a harmonium in a nearby apartment, and I have always hated that instrument ever since. These events took place in the first week in November 1894, and for many years afterward I regularly had depressive reactions every fall.

I do not know who took care of me then. My father went to work, my sister to school, and I was not allowed to stay in the house alone. I think I became a nuisance to the Braunsteins, who lived on the floor above. At some time during those dark ages, I asked my father what he did to make a living. He showed me a handful of glass pens which contained a yellow fluid, in which an orange pit was always floating to the top. He told me that he could not find work but that he peddled pens and shoe-laces in the street. His livelihood consisted of twenty-five to fifty cents a day. He also told me that many people were starving.

Now I had many reactions in which my sympathy for

my father was conspicuous. I always worried about the man who opened a new store for fear that nobody would buy anything. My heart would ache for all these people who were trying to make a living, who strove very hard and couldn't. It's still an obsession with me. I can't stand it that some people cannot make a living. The specter of want or of people out of work still haunts me.

During the winter of 1894, I was completely under my sister's care after she returned from school. Besides her, I know of no constant person who took care of me, except probably the Braunsteins. But at ten o'clock they would ask us to leave. For some unknown reason, my father did not allow us to stay alone in the three-room apartment on Orchard Street, so when the Braunsteins put us out at ten o'clock, we remained between the outer door and the inner doors of the building, in the bitter cold. My sister—herself a child—cradled me in her arms in the freezing foyer until my father returned in the small hours of the morning. We did not know that his evenings were engaged in courting our future step-mother.

On the whole, my early childhood was a ceaseless nightmare, with starvation, neglect, a sense of being of no account, and a bewildering depressive feeling. While I saw that other people "had things," I never had enough aggression to envy anyone else, a trait I have to this day.

One morning, when I was three and a half years old, my father woke me up and told me to get dressed, wash my face, and comb my hair. "At eight-thirty you will hear someone at the door. Do not be frightened. It will be a lady. She is going to be your new mother." And this is

27

what happened. She had a passkey, let herself in, and introduced herself to me. "I will be your new mother, only I don't want you to call me 'Mother.' Call me 'Auntie.' " After a preliminary look about the apartment, she remarked to me, "You look like a very nice little boy. I think I will bake you a cake." Such solicitude I had never had before, and this cake was the best I had ever eaten in my whole life.

I was immediately taken with both her manner and beauty. However, she did have a sharp tongue and constantly berated my sister and me. She claimed a higher status on the grounds that her father owned a wine tavern in Yassy, Rumania, and we were only the children of a tailor, or as she summed it up, she came from a "better class."

I survived the periodic outbursts of cruelty to my sister by my stepmother and her berating of all of us. She was honest, decent, diligent, ran the household on a pittance, and was completely dedicated to my father. My sister got the worst of it. I was her favorite, particularly after she discovered that she could not have children. I know she wanted children, because on many occasions she would invite me into her bed and insist that I fondle and suck her breasts. This was indeed strong stimulus to a child of four. For I remained passionately attached to her but not without a bit of mistrust and a constant feeling of being a nobody.

I was not then in a position to appreciate what this remarkable woman did for me. She took me out of the chaos of a devastating and unstructured environment and led me into a paradise of an ordered world. She prematurely stimulated an enormous idealization of the female, which I soon passed on to my teachers in school, with each of whom I promptly fell in love. While my attitude to the female was intense, I did not before seven concretize it in the form of sexual fantasies, which were mainly preoccupied with my stepmother and about which I must have had some guilt, because I gave myself the extenuation that "she is not my mother."

My father's guilt about my mother's death took a concrete form. At three and a half years of age, and with my stepmother's agreement, I was officially appointed my mother's "kaddish" (mourner). This meant that I had to be awakened at six-thirty in the morning, dressed, and escorted to a synagogue or congregation that met at 7:15 A.M., where my sister would ask one of the elders to prompt me in the prayers for my mother, of which I remember only the first line—*Yisgadal v'yishkadash sh'me rabboh*—for I understood no Hebrew, only learned it by rote. I remember the deep snows through which my sister and I had to plow to get to the synagogue and back. I performed this ritual daily from February to November in a hypnoidal state from which I had to be roused by my stepmother. Thus did I relieve my father's guilt about my mother.

The common opinion about me was that I was a "genius" because I showed musical talent at the age of four. I was fascinated by the sounds of music as I heard them, as on Saturday mornings, when the hurdy-gurdy man came around to grind out his repertory of the then popular operas. I became the family entertainer by singing songs my father taught me. I remember being awakened out of a deep sleep to sing for company. In recognition of my interest in music, my father bought for me the first of a series of musical instruments, beginning with a ten-note piano in the key of C, followed by a zither. What I passionately wanted was a piano. My father suggested a violin, which cost five dollars, since he could not afford a piano, which cost thirty-five dollars. And so the only instrument left was my voice. I later settled for learning to play the violin until my sister was given a piano, which I taught myself to play.

Mrs. Press, a Catholic neighbor, convinced my father that my schooling should begin at five. Since the public schools did not accept children under six, I was registered in a Catholic parochial school on East Third Street, where I stayed until the following March. One morning, in a torrential rain, I went to school only to be surprised by the command uttered by the principal: "All Jews stand up!" "Get out!" was the rest of the command. This being about nine-thirty and the rain still teeming, I was afraid to go home lest my stepmother think I was playing hooky. I took refuge in a blacksmith shop next door and watched horses being shod until the noon break. Then I went home and told my stepmother that I was thrown out of school because I was Jewish. Apart from my Hebrew education, which consisted of reading, but not understanding, a foreign language, I waited until September, when I was six, at which time I was admitted to P.S. 6 at Ludlow and Delancey streets.

I was overawed, frightened, and I considered myself stupid in comparison with the other boys in the class. My report cards were all filled with D's. But I had a special difficulty acquired by contagion. My sister had great difficulty with mathematics, and since she had once been my guardian and substitute mother, if she could not learn mathematics, I argued, how could I? I never permitted myself to learn until my last year in high school.

To account for the influences that molded my inter ooto, I must briefly describe the culture in which I lived after I was three. We lived in a three-room apartment at 176 Orchard Street, on the lower East Side, in what was then the New York "ghetto." Although the population was predominantly Jewish and Catholic, the prevailing culture was Jewish and of a high order. There were two daily Yiddish newspapers of opposing political views covering not only local but national and international affairs. There were two Yiddish repertory companies presenting the classics, Yiddish, English, and Russian, as well as the living Yiddish playwrights. Novels and poems were being written, and there was an active political movement, particularly concerned with sweatshops and the plight of the workers. It was here that settlement houses and social services began. There was much emphasis on personal as well as social ethics and a tremendous investment in the ideal of education.

A particular feature of this was the Jewish theater, which produced mainly historical plays. By the time I was six, I had seen *Judith and Holofernes,* which ended with Judith appearing triumphantly with the severed head of Holofernes, dripping with blood. Women were made fearful objects to me. But in addition I saw *Hamlet,* with the title role played by Bertha Kalish, and an endless variety of morality plays.

The newspapers read by my father and stepmother

featured murder trials of Mr. Molyneux and Nan Patterson and the famous Dreyfus case. The funnies on Sundays with Foxy Grandpa and Gaston and Alphonse were what interested me.

The entire ghetto was one large bazaar filled with pushcarts on which was everything from fresh vegetables and herrings to neckties. There was the constant shouting of hucksters proclaiming their wares at bargain prices. In addition, there were butcher shops and grocery stores. Milk was delivered in large lead-lined fifty-gallon cans and dispensed with a ladle. The streets were filled with the varied odors from bakery shops, and fresh corn bread sold for three cents a good-sized loaf.

What also impressed me were the derelicts, male and female, usually drunk, lying on the sidewalks. My father would explain to me that I had the choice of becoming one of those derelicts or becoming someone like himself, an *Arbeiter*, or workingman, constantly at the mercy of the whims of the "boss." My father at this time was an alteration hand in a female apparel shop. My third choice was to become a scholar, and preferably a "doctor." This was the narrow ambit of my choices, and I am not quite sure that I ever stopped being afraid of ending up a "bum."

The means of public transportation were horse-drawn streetcars. I rarely rode in them, because they cost a nickel. Reports of those streetcars fatally crushing people who crossed the street made my venture to and from school somewhat frightening. Even so, the horses fascinated me. During the deep snows of winter, I frequently saw them beaten by cruel drivers, who would lash at them mercilessly while they sweated in the snow. "Why," I asked myself, "don't they unite and turn on their cruel masters?" This was my second encounter with social injustice. No doubt these horses behaved like my mother, who permitted herself to be beaten by my father.

If I ever had an identity crisis, it was not during adoloo cence but during childhood. The question to me was not one of sexual identity but of Jewishness. I accepted the latter but with some reluctance. I preferred Gentiles because most of my teachers were. My identity crisis was in my self-evaluation. On the one hand, some people said I was a genius. This came from what seemed to be the most unreliable sources, my Hebrew teachers and my various aunts. On the other hand, in public school, where my grades were consistently bad, my self-esteem had already been crushed by neglect, my mother's death, and only tentative acceptance of my stepmother. My father demanded only that I make no trouble, which meant to be obedient and to do as my stepmother wished. Since the only means of survival was obedience, and the threat of becoming a social outcast (bum) hung over me, I had little ground for maneuver.

I fled, therefore, into an identification with my sister. Although I was the preferred child, I took on some of her weaknesses. After all, she had not so long before been the only mother and protector I had known. From the vantage point of the younger and weaker, how could I possibly do what she could not do? Therefore my fear of arithmetic and my general sense of defeat before life. While I ultimately surpassed her, I did so with the greatest sense of guilt. I had the feeling that what I achieved was somehow at her expense. In truth, it was simply that I had more drive, which was probably due to the fact that I had only four years of these traumatic experiences, while she had twelve.

My mathematical phobia lasted up to my last year in high school. There I flunked advanced algebra. My Latin teacher in Virgil passed me in Latin although I came to the exam without having cracked a page. I read everything at sight and I handed in an abominable paper. But he did pass me—and I never forgot his forbearance.

But in mathematics I faced a crisis. I knew that if I failed a second time, my academic career would be at an end. The regulations were that one could only repeat a course once, and if one failed again, one could not graduate.

There were several circumstances that facilitated my transition from a dunce in mathematics to second in my class in calculus.

Having been unable to stop my mind from being a sieve as regards mathematics, I acquired a teacher who made it possible for me to face the material. He evidently had little confidence in himself as a teacher and the class as students. He hit upon a remarkable teaching device. At the middle of the term, he assigned one of the students problems that we had solved months before. Then there appeared a second problem from the past, then a third, fourth, fifth, until we were doing nine problems daily. Each of the students, including myself, concluded that he was drilling us in the exam questions. On the very last day, there were still nine problems. One of my friends was in another class whose teacher went through the same performance, but on the last day he presented a fresh problem. I went home and studied this problem too. But in the meanwhile, the anxiety that heretofore had prevented me from understanding these methods of calculation disappeared.

And so I was emancipated and moreover became fascinated with the entire mathematical process. When I appeared for the exam, I was not only prepared but interested. To be sure, there were ten problems in the answers to which we had all been drilled, and I acquitted myself with an exam grade of 98. From this time onward, I excelled in mathematics. This was a true case of hysterical blindness which responded to a self-preservation necessity. It was pass and succeed in this world or fail and become the derelict—the Bowery bum. I was aided in this by the drill technique which, by helping me not only to pass but to pass with such a high grade, broke through the "I can't do this" conviction. This stopped my identification with my sister, and from here on my personality developed by leaps and bounds. For the greater part, I had contempt for the academic curriculum and was largely self-taught.

I must mention some childhood phobias I had. Some I got from my sister's history textbooks. I naturally feared Indians, who were always represented in the books, profusely illustrated, with raised tomahawks, about to strike some innocent woman or child. I had a mortal dread of masks, which were worn on holidays like Purim and Thanksgiving Day. My father once took me to the Eden Museum, which was like Mme. Tussaud's London parlors filled with wax figures of famous murderers. My howls created such a disturbance in the museum that my father had to take me out. I never understood this phobia.

I also had a great fear of Italians. There were several reasons for this. One was the reputation they had for fiery tempers and the easy use of the stiletto. This reputation became a matter of fact when several such murders due to gambling quarrels took place in the very block on which I lived. Another reason was that it was dangerous for Jewish boys to go to the Italian section. An incident which happened to me personally illustrates why. I was then about eight years old and on an errand which took me into Italian territory. Two boys, about twelve years old, stopped me and demanded to know how much money I had. I said, "Two cents." "Hand it over" was the next command, and I hastened to comply. As soon as they took my money, I fled in terror. Our neighborhood was filled with such and much worse stories, and some of the Jewish boys formed block bands to protect themselves. I was not one of them. It is interesting to note that while each neighborhood had its bands of youths, they never seriously fought each other, but rather it was the Irish against the Italians and Jews, the Italians against the Irish and Jews, and so on, down the line. I feared Jack the Ripper stories even though he lived in London.

Although I did not appreciate it at the time, the advent of my stepmother altered my fate and changed my father's character. He was no longer the irritable and overwhelmed person of my earliest years. He loved and respected my "Auntie," and he became a calm and most entertaining fellow.

Freud stopped me here and said, "Did you prepare this

hour?" I replied, "No! But why do you ask?" "Because it was a perfect presentation. I mean it was, as we say in German, *druckfertig*. I will see you tomorrow." He shook my hand and I left, elated, feeling impressed with the idea, "I can really engage him." As I left, I could not wait for my next hour to begin.

I now want to tell you briefly about the rest of my education and about the people who have been, in one way or another, important to me. Except for marginal participation in street play, I was cautioned against unsavory associations with other boys, outside the family. Sam was my cousin by marriage, as well as my age peer, and therefore became an almost obligatory associate. He was my most constant companion up until the age of thirteen, when he began to show incipient signs of pathological withdrawal, yet when I dropped him, I was severely reproached by the family. I sought more lively company, particularly Louis Hausman, who remained a companion through high school, and even college and medical school. He went into neurology and became famous as a follower of Adolf Meyer. But from about age fifteen to the present (1921), I had my most rewarding friendship with Virgil Dustin Jordan, whom I met during my first year at CCNY. He became valedictorian of the class of 1912, and subsequently the founder and first chancellor of the National Industrial Conference Board, highly honored and much respected in economic circles. He was one of those who, in addition to J. M. Keynes, advised Andrew Mellon, secretary of the treasury, not to try to collect the war indemnity imposed on Germany by the Versailles Treaty. He predicted that this attempt would destroy world markets.

The tie that bound me to Jordan and Hausman was our common passion for music. We spent a great deal of time at the piano together, particularly going over the Wagner scores. We went to many concerts and operas, and here again we shared our love for Wagner. This period was the most emotionally enriching experience of my life.

The three people in my family had the greatest influence in shaping my character. Unfortunately, my natural mother's major contribution was the trauma of her death. To my sister, who was the earliest mother I had, a lifelong series of compassion and guilt. Misfortune had pursued her through her long life. No wonder. She had been through the same things I had, but over a longer period of time. She was born in Russia and was five or six when she came with my mother to America. She was crushed by perpetual misfortune beginning with an attack of smallpox shortly after birth. Her environment was confused and formless. She was a "licked" human being, and, so far as I know, enjoyed nobody's love. She was good, kind, ingratiating, but defeated. I became the favorite, and while my stepmother deferred to me, her contempt and mistreatment of my sister gave me a sense of guilt which I still carry around with me. I tried to caution my sister against marrying a man with a rheumatic heart. She had one son. I was resolved to help her as much as I could and determined to leave her my share of my father's estate. But I never had any affection for her. She claimed too little from life and got nothing. My attitude to her was also influenced by the fact that she had those character traits I least admired in myself.

My stepmother was quite another story. She was both kind and forbidding. Because she had married at twenty-eight, she felt like an old maid, a leftover, and, added to that, she felt she had married beneath her station in life. She made disparaging remarks about my mother, and claimed superiority on the grounds that her father was a merchant and we were Russian and therefore cultur-ally inferior. While I did not understand the merits of her claims, she succeeded in confirming the impression that we were beneath contempt. This claim was reit-erated on innumerable occasions, until I was about eigh-teen years old. The last time I heard that, I threatened to beat her up if she ever made such a claim again. She stopped, and I never heard anything more about her superiority.

In contrast to the systematic crushing of my self-esteem, I had a passionate attraction to her. When I was a four-year-old, she "adopted" me as her child and treated me in a seductive manner to which I gave free rein in my fantasy because "she was not my mother" in fact. She was, indeed, very beautiful, and early in life I learned to appreciate the female body. My later fetish-istic requirements of the female body were defined by her. I could not reconcile this angry being as permitting sexual embrace, or any equivalent to it. I later learned that I was wrong about that. She was a deeply sensual female, completely devoted to my father. She demonstrated what devotion to someone else entailed, but the greatest contribution she made was to give me a structured environment.

Up to the point of her arrival, I had not had a constant and reliable source of solicitude and guidance. She provided a repetitive pattern of expectations and fulfillment. For this, I in turn had to be obedient, submissive, and not a source of "trouble." With this newfound marital stability came a more active social life. There was much mutual visiting, and I began to share my parents' friends and relatives. For the first time, I received a positive response from other people. I was promoted to family entertainer because of my musical talent, especially my singing, and was praised for being "cute," "handsome," and "smart." Some of my sense of worthlessness began to dissipate. She indoctrinated me in the ideals of integrity by her own example of dealing with others.

There was one fear that haunted my feeling of security. I feared that she might have children and my special place would be usurped. My father spoke openly of wanting them, but she never did. I later learned that she could not become pregnant. She had an uncommon anatomical anomaly: an infantile uterus. This circumstance turned out to be my good fortune and her loss.

The case of my father was different. I started out being afraid—no, terrified—of him. This was undoubtedly because I saw him abuse my mother by beating her. I was probably witness to many brutal scenes between my parents. I think that my father did not love my mother. I am quite certain that my father didn't know anything about contraceptives, and that many of the quarrels were based on my mother's refusal of sex because she did not want any more children, as she was already ill. Also, there was a depression at the time, and I think that my father was a very harassed human being, who had four mouths to feed and could not make a living. This added to his irritability.

Freud stopped me and said, "You most likely identified yourself with her." This gave me pause. I thought about it for a moment, but the point he was trying to make eluded me. But I answered as best I could, "I have no such recollection, nor do I have any recollection of what she looked like." I paused for a moment waiting for comment. Freud said nothing, so I continued. I remember seeing her shrouded face in the coffin. My sister and my mother remain indelibly marked on my memory as two unfortunate human beings.

All this vanished with the advent of my stepmother. My father's character underwent a complete change when my stepmother came into the house. He never dared to beat her. She would have left him. At that point, he admonished me to be "good" when he left for work. My stepmother was also my policeman, who reported to my father what my conduct had been. She would write on my forehead "good" or "bad" with her index finger, which made it visible for the whole world to see. I was also admonished not to associate with "bad" boys, and "badness" was associated not only with stealing and lying but with ballplaying, skating, and sports in general. They were seen as distracting from reading and study, and many was the time I was threatened with abandonment or being sent "over the water," meaning to the prisons on Randall's or Riker's Island. My stepmother did this by telling my father about minor delinquencies, and he would order my things to be packed into a bundle and tied to a broomstick, and with this suspended over my shoulder, I was marched to the door. At the very last moment, my stepmother would recommend clemency after exacting a promise never to do "it" again. Thus was obedience the guide to my early years. My submission was complete and absolute—well, almost. Because once I committed a crime so horrendous that my father decided that he would have to think it over for a week before deciding what to do about it.

My father had established a savings account for me which consisted of a piggy bank kept conspicuously on a shelf in the kitchen. It was built like an iron skyscraper, and had a slot on top. Into this "bank," my father would, from time to time, deposit coins—a penny, five cents, ten cents, up to a quarter dollar. My weekly stipend was one penny delivered faithfully every Saturday morning. The treasured penny could be spent at my discretion, usually in the candy shop for two caramel sticks or two bonbons, to be consumed ritually and in concert with Sam. I must have been about seven or eight. I was going to school, and Haber's candy store was just opposite the school. The window displayed spinning tops, pencil boxes, notebooks, compasses, and so on. On the stipend of one cent a week, I could not afford to buy rubber balls, tops, or marbles, which other boys had. I therefore conceived the idea of stealing from my own piggy bank. I would slip a knife blade into the slot and coins would fall out, and so for a while I got my tops, balls, and marbles, but I had to conceal them and lost most of them.

One morning while I was at my pilfering, I heard the lock click. It was my stepmother back unexpectedly from her shopping. In a panic, I hastily shoved the piggy bank under the sofa. Unfortunately for me, she was a meticulous cleaner, and a few days later, while I was at school, she found the hidden bank. She said nothing to me, waiting for me to note the absence of the piggy bank from its customary place. In the evening, she told my father. When confronted with the crime, I confessed. Waiting a week for the verdict was probably the longest vigil of my life. By this time, my cousins Rose and Lizzie had heard of my crime and the impending trial, and they acted as my legal defense. My defense was that one cent a week was too little to keep abreast of what other boys had. My defenders insisted that I was right. My father figured that I had stolen a dollar and twenty-five cents, but he did not punish me. He merely exacted a promise from me that if I ever felt the need for something, I was to ask him for it. I never stole again. I kept my word and so did he. Expiation by punishment would have been less effective.

My father was a remarkable raconteur. He used my sister and me as an audience and was in great demand when we went to visit others. Thus, while my environment was unstructured before three and a half, after that I was locked into a corral of obedience and incredible dependence on both parents, with no aggressive outlets except explosive outbursts of temper or sullen depressive moods. I must have had outbursts, because my father often predicted that I would end up in the electric chair. But even these occasional tantrums were denied me by the threat of fearful retaliation and by my abject dependence on my father.

Within this framework, I admired my father for his extraordinary exploits. His venture to the United States was a risky and daring undertaking in 1884. He had a great deal of courage, and under the influence of my stepmother became a devoted father and allowed me full development of my potentialities within the limits he prescribed, namely, no overt aggression.

From the time I was five years old, my father began to indoctrinate me into the objectives of education. His aim was that I achieve "respectability," which meant middle-class status. The two avenues by which this could be attained were by having enough capital to be "one's own boss," an entrepreneur, or through the professions. His choice for me was the professions, and of these he selected medicine. I agreed without any protest, and it became my fixed goal.

By the time I had reached twenty, I had three points left for my B.A. degree from City College of New York. I sought out the admissions officer at Cornell University Medical School at Twenty-eighth Street and First Avenue. My choice of Cornell as opposed to Columbia was dictated by the fact that there was a fifty-dollar difference in tuition. Though my father's financial position had improved a good deal by now, I did not want to take advantage of his largesse. I told the admissions officer my predicament and asked whether I could be admitted pending the three points for my degree in February.

In a few days, I got his answer. "If you arrange to get your degree in February of 1912, by taking a three-point course on Monday, Wednesday, or Friday, it can be arranged. Those afternoons I give the course in histology, and if you promise to make up the work, I shall not notice your absences from class." And so it was. I entered the first year of medical school, and I can truly say it was the happiest year of my life. I had a photographic memory, learned with great facility, worked hard, and from the dunce I had been in public school, I found myself at the head of my class.

The summer of 1912, after my first year in medical school, I haunted the library at 135th Street for another reason besides reading.

One of the librarians who frequently checked out my books attracted me, and I spent long hours each day just watching her move about. I fell in love with her, but how was I to make overtures to her? One day, there was no one else at the desk. I picked up a book (Renan's *Life of Jesus*) and rushed to her. In a determined way, I said, "I am interested in you. Is there any way in which I can see you outside the library?" She blushed, and after a pause said, "I could find a way, but what would my father say?" "Why not ask him?" said I.

The following morning, I started out at 8 A.M. toward St. Nicholas Avenue, and I saw her on 139th Street walking to work. I was abreast of her. "Come on along," she said. "I know your name. Mine is K——.

It's quite all right. I've noticed you many times." "What made you even think about the possibility of taking up with me?" I queried. "It was your voice. You have a very engaging voice and manner, and I liked you." This was Thursday. "May I take you home from the library on Saturday night?" "Yes, at nine." And this was the beginning. From then on, I came out every day to escort her to and from the library until school began; after that it was only Wednesday and Saturday evenings.

She was my sole preoccupation. I was in love and embarked on a disastrous course of ceaseless agony for many years to come. She had an extraordinarily beautiful face and a most graceful figure. She was also a reserved person and not much of a conversationalist. She obsessed me day and night. I visited her home, declared my love. She did not object.

By that time I had begun my second year of medical school, and became an assistant in the department of physiology under Dr. Murlin, who had a great deal of affection for me. The previous week, I had been notified by the Board of Education that I qualified as a teacher of English to foreigners. It paid three dollars an evening, or twelve dollars a week, the first money I had ever earned. This was quite a load to carry. Moreover, I had to run a research project in the physiology department after school hours and on Saturdays and Sundays. I am bringing this up to emphasize that I was under terrific pressure during this courtship. I also could not quite understand my frantic pursuit of her in view of the fact that I knew I was in no position to marry her.

On Saturday, November 2, I escorted her home as

usual. As we were walking, she had a letter in her hand and insisted on mailing it herself. As we approached her house on West 152nd Street, she said to me, "I'm afraid I will not be able to see you any more, because the letter I just mailed was an acceptance of an offer to marry. So I hope you will understand." I was stunned by the news. I hardly knew what to say, and so I just blurted out, "But I am in love with you!" To this day, I cannot forget the astonished expression on her face. I turned away and walked home in complete despair.

By the time I got home, I was in a state of desperation, and the only thing I could think of coherently was to kill myself. I did not sleep a wink that night. I got up the next morning with only one thing clear to me. Nothing mattered any more, and I was determined to shake myself free of the enormous load of work as a student and a laboratory assistant. I walked into my father's bedroom—he was not fully clad—and I blurted out, "I'm sorry to bring you bad tidings, but I am discontinuing medical school. I know how much you have helped me, but I must stop."

He was shocked by the news, but he said much less than I expected. "But why are you doing this?" "That, Dad, I just can't tell you, but my mind is made up."

I sought out my friend Jordan. He was not at home. I wandered aimlessly over the city. It was the most overwhelming despair I had ever experienced.

Monday evening, I went to my teaching assignment. On Wednesday morning, there was a letter from K—— to the effect that she had just received a letter from her fiancé advising her that he did not mind her keeping her friends in New York, because he was meaning to keep his in Chicago. In addition, she invited me to see her home from the library on Saturday evening. (I worked Wednesday evenings.) But instead of waiting that long, I went out to meet her in the morning to take her to the library.

It was a painful meeting. She said she did not know that I was in love with her until she saw how I acted on the previous Saturday. I told her I had dropped medical school. To this she remarked, "I wish you had not done that." On a subsequent occasion, she told me what she meant by that. "If you had stayed in medical school, I would have considered marrying you, but when you quit, I saw that I had to give that idea up." In short, my reaction to her engagement cost me her continued interest. No matter what I did in regard to her always turned out to be wrong.

Her family began to have objections to my continuing to see her, and so we set a deadline: January 1913. I took her to a performance of *Parsifal*. She had no real interest in music or, for that matter, in anything else, but I evidently found her quite fascinating. We walked a long way uptown from the opera house, and I said something to her I never forgot: "I do not know what kind of life I'm going to have, but when the moment comes for me to die, you will be the last thing I shall remember of this earth." I kissed her.

The following Monday morning, I was out to meet her as usual. "I'm glad you came," she said. I spent my days writing letters to her, writing scenarios for motion pictures, and several plays, not one of which was accepted. One afternoon, I received an unexpected visit from her mother, who admonished me to stop seeing K——. There was a veiled threat, but I went on seeing her anyhow, until June 1913. She told me then that she was going through with her marriage to S——. She never did. At the time she parted with me in June, she had broken her engagement because her fiancé had been named corespondent in a divorce suit. She re-engaged herself to him six months later, and then broke the second engagement.

But I kept on writing to K——, never getting a reply. On Saturday mornings, I still haunted the street where she lived, but never saw her.

One day, on May 15, 1915, I went to Fleischmann's on Fifth Avenue and ordered two dozen roses for K——'s birthday. That Saturday morning, she appeared at the usual place. "I know you've been haunting the streets around here." "You saw me?" "Yes." She was different. She had lost weight, walked faster, and there was a stony expression on her face and determination in her gait. "Your mother?" "She died." "Please tell me what it is that you have against me?" "Nothing at all, but you belong to a period of my life that I want to forget and I mean to do just that. I'm sorry that you are a victim of this circumstance." When we reached 145th Street, she said, "I'm late this morning and I will have to take the car." I tried to drop a coin in the box for her, but she forced my hand away and dropped her own nickel. "You won't take my nickel, and you surely don't take my love." Before I left her, I said, "You feel you can throw away such devotion as I have for you. You must be very rich indeed. Such devotion is hard to come by. You may never get it again." *No answer*. I kept writing to her from time to time. Finally, I received a letter which told me the truth. It was to the effect that she had nothing against me, but that she had no capacity to feel anything for anyone.

The hurt of this relationship stayed with me all these many years, and up until this time. I had not been able to commit myself to any other woman.

In January 1914, I registered for a doctorate at Columbia University in the Department of Anthropology and Philosophy. I became acquainted with John Dewey and took his unforgettable course in logic. I also became acquainted with Franz Boas and Alexander Goldenweiser. Both were severe critics of the evolutionary anthropologists, particularly Frazer. I learned a little Sanskrit and read the Bhagavad-Gita in the original language. At the end of the term, I decided that academic life was not for me.

Since I had left medicine only to devote all my time to courting K——, and since this courtship had ended in failure, I decided to return to the other love in my life—medicine.

I then wrote the dean of Cornell Medical School, who advised me that I could come back and that my scholarship was assured. I saw Dr. Murlin, and he welcomed me back. I answered that I owed him an apology. "Do you remember, when I discontinued, you asked me, 'Was there a woman mixed up in this?' " "Yes," he answered. "Well, you were right."

I thoroughly enjoyed the next three years of medical

school, graduated with top honors, and received an internship at Mount Sinai Hospital.

Freud had listened to my whole story without even once breaking in to comment. Now, however, he spoke. "Your reaction to the breakup with K—— was unfortunately, as they say, 'in the cards.' Her treatment of you was a repetition of your reaction to the death of your mother. It left you confirmed in your feeling of worthlessness, abandonment, and depression. However bad your reaction was, I can say to you—and let this be a guide to your future—You may be down, but you will never be out." I felt very much encouraged by Freud's observation. I evidently had more strength than I gave myself credit for. Freud gave me a much needed boost!

My twenty-one-month internship at Mount Sinai was likewise a very happy time, notwithstanding the great epidemic of 1918 and the war. However, one of the saddest days of my life was the day my internship ended. My carefree days were over, I had no plans, no money, and no prospects. I had a great interest in psychiatry, but those psychiatrists I knew were in the service of the state hospitals. A career as an employee of a state hospital did not sound like a very promising career to me. After working for one week with an internist, doing urinalysis, blood counts, and histories, I decided that this too was no future for me.

The physicians who might have been of help were still in the European war theater, and none of the remaining surgeons needed new assistants. So, notwithstanding a very effective internship and having graduated as house surgeon, I was unable to find a job.

I had read a book, *Morbid Fears and Compulsions*, by

H. W. Frink and was much impressed with it. Here was a branch of medicine that was independent of state hospitals and in which one could establish a private practice. Above all, I became fascinated by the whole field involving the mysteries of the human mind. I went to see Dr. Horace W. Frink, my teacher in neurology at medical school. In my interview with Frink, he told me two things that decided my future. One was that psychiatry was the wave of the future, and the other was that anyone could make a great discovery. What could be more adventurous than to be a Columbus in the relatively new science of the mind?

I then asked, "How does one go about getting into this new field?" Frink answered, "Get a job in a state hospital so you can learn to identify the important psychiatric syndromes; second, you must undertake a personal analysis." "And to whom do I go for that?" Frink replied, "To me!"

And so I agreed to see him three times weekly and also began as a resident at Manhattan State Hospital under Mortimer Raynor and August Hoch, two great clinicians.

At that time, I knew nothing about what went into a therapeutic session. Hence, I went in without any foreboding or fear, but very soon after I began I found myself scared and frightened. I was apparently protecting myself against some unidentifiable danger.

One day, I was reminiscing about my childhood, and I remembered some of the then popular songs, one of which was "Sweet Isaac Ben Bolt." To which Frink remarked, "You mean 'Sweet Alice, Ben Bolt.'" I had substituted my father's name for the ballad's dead Alice. "It's obvious that you wanted your father to die," said Frink.

The next hour, I continued to tell the story of my analysis with Frink and how I had begun to dread my visits with him.

His statement about my wishing my father dead had an immediate and devastating effect on me. My impression was that my father was my rock of ages, my dependence on him inordinately strong, and yet I wanted him to die? "Why?" I asked Frink. The answer came at once. "It was that you envied him the possession of your stepmother." This revelation, that I wanted this man whom I consciously adored dead, devastated me. I did not dispute this interpretation because I felt that I had no authority to do so, but I left the hour in a state of anxiety. What frightened me most was that I could entertain ideas of which I had no awareness. For many sessions thereafter, my discomfort continued, and I had only one clear objective. I wanted out of this analysis as quickly as I possibly could. I was certain that as soon as it stopped, so would my discomfort.

In this atmosphere of resistance, guilt, and general feeling of "How did I get into this mess?" I had a very dramatic dream, which puzzled both Frink and me. Freud, however, made some sense out of it, although I am not sure, even now, that I fully understand it.

I was in a cellar in which there were a great many old articles of furniture that had been discarded because of age or because they were broken. They were in disorderly array. A balcony overhung the right side of the cellar, and on this balcony were standing three Italians with their penises exposed, and they were urinating on me. I felt very humiliated and downcast. I woke up in a depressed state. It was Saturday morning and I was due at a staff meeting. Several patients were brought in and discussed. The last of these was a Negro. The only thing I remember about him is that he looked dilapidated, and Dr. Raynor said he had an unusual symptom for a schizophrenic—he had lost his "memory." And with this, a chill ran through me. "By God, the same thing could happen to me!" I was very uncomfortable, and after another ten minutes, when the meeting was over, I went up to Dr. Raynor and asked permission not to go back to work that afternoon. I went to my room and went to sleep. I had a second dream.

I was in bed with my stepmother. I was having intercourse with her, but there was something unusual about it. I felt as if I was ripping something up as I inserted. I woke up.

I said to Freud, "Frink could not help me much with these dreams. I hope you can."

Freud: "What associations about them can you tell me?"

"There was only one thing. When I was very young, my father used to tell me apocryphal stories about biblical characters. One that stood out prominently in my mind was about Jesus. He was regarded as a bastard, a trickster and flimflammer. One day, he went to the Holy of Holies and stole from it the 'Schema Phoresh,' which had some magical inscription on it. It was apparently either a talisman or a piece of holy scripture. He took it, opened the skin of his leg, and sewed it into the flesh. With this magical power, he began to fly around, demonstrating his supernatural powers. The high priest saw this and decided to expose Jesus as a fake. He also went to the holy place and took the 'Schema Phoresh' and also sewed it into his flesh. He also began to fly in the sky, but he flew higher than Jesus. While he was over him, the high priest pissed on Jesus, and that robbed him of his magical power. He fell to the earth, humiliated and exposed. As for my associations to Italians, in the neighborhood in which I grew up Italians were considered murderers, quick with the stiletto."

Freud: "This is indeed a very interesting dream, and you did quite a bit of condensation in a few seconds of dreaming. The cellar with the discarded furniture simply means a long time ago, when you were a little boy; things discarded are the past. The Italians were those you most feared. Three Italians equal one big Italian, your father. You felt small, humiliated, outdone by your father and belittled by him. What the amnestic Negro you saw in staff was, was a projection into the future of what you actually feared in the past. What you feared was therefore not what was going to happen but *what actually had happened*, and which you not only forgot, *but feared to recall*. And what you feared with Frink was that if he knew of your murderous intentions toward your father, he would withdraw his love and support, as you once feared your father would. And what you feared was the return of your sense of humiliation which devastated your childhood.

"But I see from your second dream that you are not

necessarily willing to surrender. You do have intercourse with your stepmother. That's the assertive part of your character and part of your masculine protest. There's a lot of fight in you. It was a life-or-death struggle for your survival. You undoubtedly felt very insignificant in your childhood."

I continued associating. "My stepmother taught me to appreciate women, and she did behave in a seductive manner to me between my fourth and seventh years. The extenuation for my ardent fantasies was that "she is not my mother, and therefore fair prey." Freud said, "There was nothing unconscious about it. It's a manifestation of the Oedipus complex."

Freud then proceeded to clarify my fears aroused by my analysis with Frink. "The analysis itself merely opened up your old latent fears of abandonment and your inability to be assertive with your father. This was the conflict that was the issue in the Frink analysis; namely, how dared you to compete with the man whose favor and support you wanted, and who you were afraid would humiliate you if you disclosed your competitiveness with him—to displace him, especially with your stepmother. In the dream of intercourse with your stepmother, you try to handle these anxieties in a more assertive way."

Now, where Frink could not proceed from this dream, it acted as a catalyst for the remainder of my analysis with Freud, because this dream led directly to my childhood relations with my father. It was quite obvious although I was not fully aware of it.

So far, Freud seemed to be on the right track. He had

already warned me that my relations to my father were "retouché," and that I feared him but coveted my step-mother. He was also right in recognizing that her be-havior to me was provocative, and while it stimulated my aggressive fancies about her, it also augmented my guilt toward my father, on whom I was so dependent. This was my neurosis.

He dismissed me with this. It was the end of the hour and I left in a very agitated and disturbed frame of mind. I was not prepared for anything like this. Having heard the interpretation of this enigmatic dream of the three urinating Italians, I was very bewildered by the proceedings.

That night I had a dream. In this dream, I was stand-ing on an embankment. Two or three men were digging a trench. I was very exercised over their activities, and I kept importuning them to please stop digging, saying that they would find nothing of any value, that they would find nothing but an old rag. Finally, in the dream, they did come up with a rag, and I said, "You see! There isn't anything there." That is where this episode in the dream ended. My association to this dream was with Guy de Maupassant's short story called "La Ficelle." It was about the loss of a valuable necklace and an old man who bent down to pick something up from the street with-out seeing the necklace lying there in the gutter. He was arrested and accused of stealing the necklace, and this poor old man kept protesting, "But you don't understand. . . . All I did was pick up a piece of string."

Then there was another dream, I think the same night,

which I never did understand thoroughly. I was alongside an enormous cat whom I apparently was not afraid of, but who was unmoving and indifferent.

Freud said, "Well, apparently we hit something very important here. In the first dream, you obviously don't want me to pursue your relationship with your father. You want the picture to remain as you retouched it, and so, in the dream, you tell me not to go digging up the past, I will not find anything important."

"But why," I asked, "did I retouch the picture of my father?"

"To make it possible for you to live with him at all. You evidently were terrified of him in your very early childhood. However, when your stepmother came, your father's character changed, and it is this revised character you wished to keep and thereby to forget the angry father of your earliest years. But you remained submissive and obedient to him in order not to arouse the sleeping dragon, the angry father." My immediate reaction was to accept Freud's interpretation. It was not until many years later that I understood the basic error committed here by Freud.

The man who had invented the concept of transference did not recognize it when it occurred here. He overlooked one thing. *Yes, I was afraid of my father in childhood, but the one whom I feared now was Freud himself.* He could make me or break me, which my father no longer could. By his statement, he pushed the entire reaction into the past, thereby making the analysis a historical reconstruction. The "retouché" part of his interpretation, however, was quite correct.

I had been more afraid of and more submissive to my father than I was aware and had also concealed from myself my own aggression and hostility to him. But for the same reasons, I was now afraid to have Freud discover my concealed aggression. I made a silent pact with Freud. "I will continue to be compliant provided that you will let me enjoy your protection." If he rejected me, I would lose my chance to enter this magical professional circle. This tacit acceptance on my part sealed off an important part of my character from scrutiny.

"The cat," I said. "What about the cat?" "The big cat," Freud replied, "that is your stepmother."

This set off a train of associations in my mind. I could still see the enigmatic expression on the cat's face. It seemed immovable, unapproachable, indifferent. What did that have to do with my stepmother? While I feared my father, I lacked "trust" in her. Maybe that was the connection with the cat. Would she be there when I really needed her, especially as a protector against my father? The answer seemed to be in the cat. She was not hostile but immobile!

Out loud, I said to Freud, "But my stepmother was such a stabilizing force in my life that I will always be grateful to her."

For the first time in the analysis, Freud raised his voice. "You are mistaken about your stepmother. While it is true that she gave you a structured environment, she also overstimulated you sexually and thereby augmented your guilt toward your father. You took refuge from this dilemma by fleeing into your unconscious homosexuality by way of identification with your natural mother. The basis for this was that you identified yourself with your helpless mother, for fear of identifying yourself with the enraged, aggressive father."

I tried to relate to what Freud was telling me. I could understand the identification and the female part. As a child, I remember feeling that it was an extraordinary privilege to be one of these remarkable creatures. They seemed to have so much easier a time of it. All they had to do was take care of the house and the children. The real responsibility was on the father. Having watched my father's efforts to make a bare living, that picture was understandable. In looking at this grown-up giant of a man and seeing his struggles, I, the child, could only feel an ego weakness that made me unequal to the task of performing exploits of great daring, like coming to America or combating a hostile world to eke out a livelihood. So my wish for the female role was really a wish to escape the hardships of being a male. But this had never interfered with my erotic drive toward the female. Therefore Freud's interpretation took me aback. I could not understand what all this had to do with unconscious homosexuality, and I asked Freud to explain.

"What do you mean," I asked Freud, "by unconscious homosexuality?"

He explained, "By identifying himself with the mother, the child surrenders his identification with the father, thereby discontinuing his role as rival to the father. This guarantees him the continued protection of the father, thereby answering his dependency needs."

"What can I do about this?"

Freud's answer was, "Well, just as with the Oedipus

complex, you come to terms with it. You reconcile yourself to it."

In comparing notes with other students, I discovered that, as with the Oedipus complex, unconscious homosexuality was a routine part of everyone's analysis. It consumed a good part of the rest of my analysis.

I had left the last hour feeling quite calm but somewhat intrigued by these new insights. But apparently the material having to do with my association with the female began to stir things up a bit, and I had a dream about a mask, from which I awoke with great apprehension. The dream stimulated very important associations which led to the discovery of a childhood phobia that I had had, namely, the fear of masks and clothed wax figures. Freud asked, "What was there about the mask that frightened you so?" My first response was that it was the facial immobility, the lack of expression, the fact that it neither smiled nor laughed, and that the face was immobile. I myself had had several dreams in which I could see myself in the mirror, and the face would not reflect my emotional expression; that is, I would smile or I would frown, but the expression in the mirror did not change.

Freud drew the conclusion that the possibility was that "the first mask you saw was your dead mother's face." Now, this idea sent shivers through me when I first thought about it, but the circumstantial evidence from this dream and the associations led to the striking possibility that I had discovered my mother dead, while I was alone with her in the house.

I told Freud, "Well, if you wanted any evidence for

the basis of identification with my mother, here it is. I was, in all likelihood, alone with her when she expired. There was also a superstition popular at that time that if you were with someone who died, you would breathe in the soul of that person, which was expelled with his last breath." When I returned to New York, my sister confirmed this. She was old enough to remember the events very accurately because she was at that time eleven years old, and she told me what had happened. She said that nothing unusual had happened on that day, because my mother was chronically ill and she was left home alone. I was with her, playing on the floor. Apparently, I wanted something and I shook her. She did not respond or answer, and I was frightened. When my sister came home for lunch, she discovered that my mother was dead and that I was alone in the room crying.

"Well," said Freud, "it's obvious from your associations that the mask represented your mother's dead face. Therefore, all masks or wax figures were associated with death, and brought back the old terror."

At the end of the fifth month, March, he began saying, "Herr Doktor, ein bischen Durcharbeitung [working through]." Now, this idea caused me a good deal of bewilderment. I had no idea what he meant, and I begged him to elucidate what he meant by *Durcharbeitung*. He said, "Well, why don't you bring your childhood neurotic manifestations into your current life?"

I did not know at the time that this was the main job of analysis, but I did say to Freud, "I thought that was your job." However, at that time Freud didn't consider it to be so. He thought that once you had uncovered the

Oedipus complex and understood your unconscious homosexuality, that once you knew the origins and the sources of all these reactions, something would happen that would enable you to translate these insights into your current life and thereby alter it.

However, as for me, at the time his invitation that I should work through this whole thing only left me bewildered. From this point on, the analysis drifted. In this period, I only remember having two dreams.

My first dream was an endless plainlike Russian steppe —covered with snow. My association to this was the snow common in early childhood, and my going to and from the synagogue to say kaddish for my mother, when I was three and a half years old. It was always through deep snows.

My second dream was of the console of the organ in the main hall at CCNY, which was in one position, and then in the same dream it was in another position—turned around. My association was that I was very fond of the music played by Professor Baldwin at City College, whose recitals I used to attend; I would come an hour earlier to school just to hear him rehearse, and this is where I learned to love Bach. One piece of music, "Benedictus," by Max Reger, a prominent German composer of the day, intrigued me no end.

Freud made no comments about either dream except to say that snow dreams indicate a depressive mood, which must appertain to my mother's death, and to this day I still have no idea what they mean.

3

Freud as Analyst

SOMETIME in early March, Freud told me that my analysis would terminate on April 1. I was very much disturbed by this and protested vehemently, but Freud would not be moved. When he reminded me that he had stipulated a six-month period in his original letter to me, I was even more shocked. I had not forgotten it; I had never really seen it. It had simply not registered with me.

But in the meanwhile, I discovered that Frink was coming back to Freud for more analysis, and this disturbed me. I had been counting on him to be my sponsor in New York and to launch me on my new career. When I mentioned some of this to Freud, he said, "You once said that analysis couldn't hurt anyone. Well, let me show you something." He took out two photographs. "One of these is Frink before analysis, and the other is after one year of analysis." I was shocked at what I saw. In the first photograph, he looked as I had known him. In the second, he was haggard, emaciated, and looked twenty years older. What neither Freud nor I knew at this time was that the drastic change in Frink was due not to the analysis but to other causes.

My analysis terminated on the first of April 1922. I felt uneasy, reluctant to leave, and, in a way, resentful about it. I asked Freud for an autographed photograph, which he gave me. On it he wrote in German, "To Dr. A. Kardiner—as a friendly remembrance of his sojourn in Vienna—Freud." The rest of the hour we just chatted, I cannot remember about what, but when I was leaving, he said, "I wish you well and hope that someday you will have the good fortune to make a good marriage," and as a last word, "Someday you will be a wealthy man." I still do not know why he added that. I had been waiting for him to make some comment about the analysis, hoping, of course, that he would have glowing things to say, or that at the very least he would pull things together, sum it all up in some way. None of this happened. However, when I next saw him, in the summer of 1927, he greeted me with "Ah, Herr Doktor, Sie haben wass von Ihre Analyse gelernt." Translated: "You really learned something from your analysis."

By then, however, this came as no great surprise, because when I returned to New York in 1922, Frink told me he had received several letters from Freud, and that, judging from what he wrote, he was highly pleased. Frink showed me an excerpt from one he received when my analysis was finished, which read as follows: "Kardiner's analysis is complete and perfect. He ought to have a great career." Needless to say, I was pleased to hear this, but somehow wished that Freud could have told me this when we were parting.

As for the evaluation of Freud as an analyst, at that time I was much too close to the experience to appraise what had happened. I once asked Freud what he thought of himself as an analyst. "I'm glad you ask, because, frankly, I have no great interest in therapeutic problems.

I am much too impatient now. I have several handicaps that disqualify me as a great analyst. One of them is that I am too much the father. Second, I am much too much occupied with theoretical problems all the time, so that whenever I get occasion, I am working on my own theoretical problems, rather than paying attention to the therapeutic problems. Third, I have no patience in keeping people for a long time. I tire of them, and I want to spread my influence," which is probably why he kept many people for only short periods of time.

It was quite clear to me that the skeletal outline of the analysis was the Oedipus complex. The accommodations to it consumed most of the time, but it is very important to note that he did not use the libido theory. He did not talk about anal eroticism except in passing, and there were several dreams that I had toward the end of the analysis in which there was some discussion of this, but it hardly made a part of the scheme that Freud used in integrating the whole neurotic structure. In other words, the analysis was taken up with the Oedipus complex, the derivation of the dependency constellation, with its unconscious homosexuality, as one of the resolutions of the failures to resolve the Oedipus complex satisfactorily, in which state Freud found me.

However, as can be seen from the few examples I have given, Freud was brilliant at dream interpretation and was very intuitive in interpreting free associations.

Freud was always infuriated whenever I would say to him that you could not do harm with psychoanalysis. He said, "When you say that, you also say that it cannot do any good. Because if you cannot do any harm, how can you do good?" Yet, as with many other things, he could be humorous and somewhat irreverent about psychoanalysis.

Monroe Meyer and I once discussed with Freud the suicides of two analysts in Vienna. His eyes twinkling, he commented, "Well, the day will soon come when psychoanalysis will be considered a legitimate cause of death."

Freud had a great fear about the future of psychoanalysis. He believed that psychoanalysis would founder because it would go down in history as a "Jewish" science. He hated this idea. He said this was a preoccupation with him and that he did not know what to do about it, because most of the people who were attracted to it were Jewish. Some of this anxiety was realized, but the greatest irony was when Jung, in a Swiss psychoanalytic journal in 1942, labeled psychoanalysis "a Jewish science."

A good deal of time during analysis was taken up with small talk about my colleagues, and occasionally there was some gossip on Freud's part, such as that he was unequivocally opposed to Oberndorf because he proved skeptical and refractory in accepting interpretations. On the other hand, he spoke about Alfred Adler, Stekel, and others. Freud's own comment about Adler was that he was too proud to live in the shadow of this giant, meaning himself. This was Freud's attempt to minimize Adler's introduction into psychoanalytic theory of the concept of masculine protest, feeling of inferiority, and sense of identity. Yet Freud had used this idea of masculine protest as part of the interpretation of my dream of sexual intercourse with my stepmother. The only one he did not talk about was Jung. He refused on the grounds that it was too painful to him both personally and scientifically.

In our hours together, there were many personal interchanges. I was enormously fond of him. This was a very likable and dear person. He was a charming man, full of wit and erudition. One could not tell from his behavior in the office what a real giant he was, because he was unassuming and quite natural.

I said to him many times in the course of the analysis, "I can't reconcile the image I get of you in this room with the man who wrote all those great books."

His reply to that was, "This is where familiarity breeds contempt."

But in addition to the extraordinary perspicacity, the great breadth of this man's vision, the fact that he himself was so much in control of a great movement made itself felt, particularly when he was in public. I saw this aspect of him at the meetings of the Vienna Psychoanalytic Society, where this man seemed like a giant among pygmies. And I must say, at this point, that at no time in my entire contact with the psychoanalytic movement, and all the people that were in it, did I meet anybody besides Freud who qualified as a genius. Whatever errors he made, there is no question of the scope of this man's vision, of the way in which this man, if he did not lead us into the Promised Land, at least certainly opened the doors.

I think he was quite aware of his fame and importance, but when asked whether he considered himself a great man, he would always modestly say, "I don't think so, but I made a great discovery."

That he did not take himself or his fame too seriously is illustrated by the following story. I lived with a family by the name of Frankel, on the Essling Gasse, in the First District. The Frankels were middle-class, well-to-do people who had invested their money, like all good Austrians, in government bonds, and after World War I these were totally worthless. So these people had to take boarders in order to eke out a living and to help pay their rent. These rents were all government controlled, and my apartment—furnished—cost me three dollars (American equivalent) per month. I had a living room and a bedroom and maid service for the equivalent of nine thousand crowns. Add to that the heating wood, which was extra, and the electricity, and the rent came to about ten dollars a month. My sojourn in Vienna was the only time in my entire life when I was a rich man, when the dollar bought three thousand crowns or more—and you can imagine what the crown was worth (or, rather, how much the dollar bought) if a good meal was seventy-five crowns and a ticket to the opera in the orchestra cost sixteen cents. I was a millionaire with a few hundred dollars in my pocket.

My host, Mr. Frankel, who probably wanted to make sure that he was not harboring an international criminal of some kind, came to me one day to ask how I was enjoying my stay in Vienna, and what I was doing there. He wanted particularly to know that.

I told him I was a physician and that I was studying with Professor Freud.

"Professor Freud?" he asked. "I never heard of any such professor." I said, "He's a professor at the university." He said, "That's strange. My son-in-law is a professor of gynecology at the university, and I know all the professors, but I never heard of Professor Freud, but the name does sound a little familiar to me. Just wait a minute, I have an idea." And he disappeared from the room, returned about a minute later, thumbing the pages of a little blue book, and read down the list. He said, "Freud, Sigmund, Berggasse 19? Ach, he's a lodge brother of mine!"

The little book from which he was reading was the list of members of the B'nai B'rith of the city of Vienna.

The next day, I hastened to tell this story to Freud, and he thought it was a great joke. He said, "You see? A prophet is never known in his own country." Furthermore, the Frankels lived just three blocks away from Freud.

Another anecdote illustrates Freud's laconic, pithy way of illuminating a situation, his incredible sense of humor in what looked like a catastrophe.

Shortly before I left Vienna, one of my colleagues got into trouble with his wife. He had been keeping company with a young girl. He once asked me whether I would be kind enough to spend an evening with her. I was to listen to her playing and evaluate her prospects as a violin virtuoso, in which my colleague was prepared to make a considerable investment.

So I went there and heard her give a most mediocre performance. At the same time, I appraised her personality too. I told another of my colleagues, who knew I had visited her, what I thought. I told him, "No talent, and as a personality, no affect."

Within a day or so, I met the girl's sponsor. My advice was, "Don't make any investment in her talent. It is non-existent."

Meanwhile, his wife in New York got wind of the fact that her husband was running around with a younger and more attractive woman. Suddenly she appeared in Vienna and confronted her husband. He had always boasted to me and to the others about his sexual prowess. However, when his wife arrived—after he was discharged by Freud—he discovered that he was impotent. After a few more trials, he went into a panic. "What? Impotent *after* analysis?" His despair was beyond control, and he finally decided to write to Freud for an appointment, since Freud could never be reached by phone, and gave a brief description of his embarrassing situation. Freud gave him an appointment and listened to his story. He thought Freud would wring his hands and take him back into analysis. Instead, Freud did not utter a word during the entire interview, and when his hour was up, he rose, seized my friend's hand with the usual handshake, and said, "Und jetzt sehe ich dass Sie ein wirklich und anständiger Kerl sind" (Well, now I see that you are a really decent fellow!), and ushered him out.

All of the gang still remaining in Vienna were called together to meet at a café on the Währingerstrasse to discuss what the meaning of Freud's laconic utterance was.

The discussion went on for hours, but we finally came to a plausible conclusion. What Freud meant was this: Up to now—i.e., before your analysis—you were a bit of a scoundrel, but since your analysis you at least have the decency to be impotent with the woman you betrayed. So this impotence is witness to the fact that you have undergone a change of character—for the better.

And thus ended the conference. He regained his potency when he gave up the girl, who then went into a psychotic break.

This story is testimony to Freud's self-possession and how he could condense a whole sermon into a single sentence. I saw no evidence of any great arrogance in this man. On the contrary, I saw a certain control and self-assurance, but he knew that he was in command of an important movement, and everybody else in the movement kowtowed to him. He demanded absolute loyalty. He regarded it as his privilege to say to me one day, when I was discussing his theory of primal parricide, "Oh, don't take that too seriously. That's something I dreamed up on a rainy Sunday afternoon."

But then again, if you did not take it seriously, your head would come off. I didn't know which way it was. "Well," he would say, "this was just an idea"; but if you opposed him, you got into serious trouble. The following story illustrates what could happen if you incurred Freud's wrath.

Clarence Oberndorf was one of my fellow American students. He didn't seem to me to be a very neurotic man, and though he was no great intellect, he was a persistent plodder and a most agreeable person to work with. He had been one of my teachers at Cornell, as well as my chief at the Mount Sinai Clinic, and he was one of the people who had fascinated me with the whole subject of psychiatry. Oberndorf got to be on bad terms with Freud on the very first day of his analysis, because he came prepared with a dream, which he related in the very first hour. The dream was as follows: He was riding in a carriage pulled by two horses, one of which was white, and the other black. They were going to some unknown destination.

Traveling to an unknown destination as an opening dream in analysis is not infrequent. But this particular dream happened, rightly or wrongly, to hit upon one of Oberndorf's apparent weak spots, because it was Freud's interpretation that he, Oberndorf, could never marry because he didn't know whether to choose a white woman or a black woman, and so he was in a quandary. He was not married then, nor did he ever marry, and he was a Southerner. He was born in Atlanta, Georgia, and had been raised by a black "mammy." This interpretation infuriated Oberndorf, and they haggled about this dream for months, until Freud got tired of it and discontinued the analysis. Freud was unequivocal in his condemnation of Oberndorf's character and of his ability, and later on he even refused to write a preface for a book he had written.

Freud was a good paterfamilias. He spoke about his children quite often, and I once remarked to him that at times he seemed depressed. He admitted that this was true, because his daughter Mathilda had died only a short while before I arrived in Vienna some months before, and he was very much under the influence of her death. He could not get over it, and as a matter of fact, when I left Vienna and I told him that I was going to pass through Hamburg on my way back, he asked me to please see his son-in-law and his grandchildren. I never got the opportunity to do so.

His daughter Anna was unquestionably his favorite, and she was at that time teaching school. She came to the meetings of the Vienna Psychoanalytic Society, but never spoke or participated in any discussions. She was quite an attractive girl, and, as later events proved, a chip off the old block. Rumor had it that she was being analyzed by her own father. I do not know whether this was just a rumor or whether there was some truth to it. Another rumor was that he sent her to Lou Andreas-Salomé, an analyst for whom Freud had great regard. I never met Lou, but I did ask Freud why he thought so highly of her. His reply was, "There are some people who have an intrinsic superiority. They have an inborn nobility. She is just one of those people."

All of the students surrounding Freud at that time were filled with all kinds of theories as to why Anna Freud was not married. Freud was aware that she was having difficulty choosing a husband, and when he once asked me, "Do you have any theory about why?" my answer was, "Well, look at her father. This is an ideal that very few men could live up to, and it would surely be a comedown for her to attach herself to a lesser man."

The fact that Freud talked to me excited a good deal of attention in Vienna, so much so that one day I was honored with an invitation to tea by James Strachey and John Rickman. I had no idea what they wanted, but rumor had reached them that Freud talked to me. When I asked them what this meeting was all about, John Rickman said to me, "I understand Freud talks to you."

I said, "Yes, he does, all the time."

They said, "Well, how do you do it?"

I answered, "I don't exactly know. Maybe it's the hour of the day, maybe I keep him interested, maybe I keep hopping. I don't know, but he is quite garrulous. How is it with you?"

They both said, "He never says a word." Rickman added, "I suspect he sleeps. In fact, I know he does, because I know how to wake him. I just stop talking, and after a few moments of silence, Freud jumps in with a 'Yes, yes—go on, please.' One time I even said to him, 'What I said wasn't very important, Herr Professor, so you can go back to sleep.' "

Now, since James Strachey and John Rickman agreed about his silences, I supposed they couldn't hold his interest. I said, "Well, tell me something about your analysis."

He said—this was John Rickman speaking—"It's something about an infantile fantasy that I had, and I'm stuck there, and I don't know where to go from here; and Freud doesn't seem to be able to help me with it very much."

I don't think that this conference was a big success, but I would guess that Freud's behavior with these British students gave rise to the "English" school of psychoanalysis, in which the analyst says nothing at any time other than "Good morning" and "Goodbye." And this can go on as long as four, five, or six years. I know this because I have had several people who were analyzed by English analysts of the vintage of Rickman and Jones, none of whom ever talked. In fact, I had one patient who discharged herself from analysis with the following statement: "Doctor, you haven't said a word to me since I came here six months ago. Can't I do this at home?"

4

Freud and the Psycho-analytic Movement

ABOUT A YEAR AND A HALF later when Frink returned to New York, he came with orders from Freud to revise and revitalize the then present New York Psychoanalytic Society, headed by A. A. Brill. Frink was to organize a committee to handle this renovation. When, one day, Frink announced to Oberndorf that he was not to be a member of the organizing committee, Oberndorf was infuriated. He said, "I'm one of the old-timers here. Why do you take these novices and put them in important positions and I get left out?"

Frink said, "I'm sorry, I'm following directions. Freud does not want you in."

The sad fact was that the whole economic structure of the psychoanalytic movement rested entirely on Freud's shoulders. He was the dispenser of all the favors and patients for the entire group of analysts in Vienna, and this was the source of both loyalty and corruption. To be sure, there weren't many psychoanalysts—maybe fifteen or twenty—but they all cleared through Freud, so that he had an enormous amount of control over both economic and status advancement. One should not fail to recognize that this was a corrupting influence, as it also created a great deal of rivalry, infighting, and maneuvering among his followers. It led to ingratiating oneself with the man who fed you. In fact, several of the people who were "Adlerians" came back begging to be reinstated, like Isidor Sadger and Fritz Wittels, who had become Adlerians and then turned back to the fold and became more violently orthodox than Freud himself.

A word about the group as a whole, and their behavior in Vienna. There was a good deal of indiscreet gossip among the students about Freud and everyone else in the analytic movement, but the American and English contingents were separated by an unfathomable gulf of social caste. I was the only one who was ever invited to tea, and then only because they wanted to pump me about how to get Freud's attention. Outside of that, we were all socially shunned, collectively and individually. I do not think there was anything overt about it, but we were made to feel we just did not belong.

However, we all did get together on several joint enterprises. Shortly after we got there, we had the idea of getting all those great minds with whom we were in contact in Vienna to give us some didactic courses. Freud fell in with this idea and thought it was a brilliant way of beginning. These, by the way, were the first formal teaching courses in psychoanalysis ever given in Vienna or anywhere else. Nobody had ever thought of the idea of didactic courses, and the whole concept of a supervisory analysis had not yet been invented. The training in analysis consisted of being analyzed oneself. That was all.

Didactic courses made up a good part of our entertainment and instruction. And we had the great men, all of them with the exception of Ernest Jones. He did not come, but we saw Ferenczi, Abraham, and others. Abraham gave a paper on the spider as the female genital symbol. Otto Rank gave a course of lectures on dream interpretation. Helene Deutsch gave a course on clinical psychoanalysis.

Helene Deutsch, it must be observed here, was one of the great beauties of Vienna. She looked like Helen of Troy. We all loved her very much, and she deserved it too, because she was a great teacher. Her great virtue lay in her simplicity and her very sound common sense. She was the person Freud entrusted to go to Berlin in 1924 to study and appraise the libido theory innovations Karl Abraham was making there.

I do not know what report Helene Deutsch brought back, but when I heard about the possibility of her trip, I asked Freud what he thought of the Berlin technique of using the libido theory as the framework for the "working through" process of the analysis. Freud said, "I do not know, and I am not ready to give any opinion about it. But I can only tell you this—Karl Abraham is no fool. He is the most accurate and honest worker that I have among my followers. This man not only does not waste his time, but he is the most thorough and persistent man in the whole psychoanalytic movement today. He's a man whose work should be followed and we will see. Only time will tell."

Up to then, the libido theory was used only as a frame of reference for theoretical discussions, not in the analytic therapy itself. I can only gather from ensuing events that Helene Deutsch brought back to Vienna a very favorable report about Abraham's work, because she taught it to the Viennese group and it became standard procedure. Whatever may be said about this new method, it was systematic and concrete. It gave an artificial precision to analysis which it had never had before, as one can see from Freud's analysis of me, which was quite typical of the way he worked. Once he located the Oedipus complex and worked through the unconscious homosexuality, there wasn't anything much left to do. One unscrambled the patient and let him scramble it together as best he could by himself. And if he didn't do it, Freud would give him a couple of barbs every now and then to encourage him and to hasten matters. Freud really did not know very much about *Durcharbeitung*, as we now understand it, though it subsequently became the essential task of the therapeutic process.

Hermann Nunberg gave us a course on the psychoses. Eduard Hitschmann gave us a course on the general theory of the neuroses. Isidor Sadger gave us a course on the sexual perversions. Geza Roheim inducted us into the relation of anthropology to psychoanalysis, at that time a new concept. Theodor Reik gave us a couple of lectures on similar subjects, but devoted them largely to studies in the mythology of the ancient Hebrews.

Theodor Reik trimmed his beard exactly the way Freud did, smoked the way Freud smoked, and talked the way Freud talked. We called him "the imitation Freud."

The rest of the teachers were all very instructive, but the people I most enjoyed were Helene Deutsch and Hermann Nunberg. They were very good clinical teachers.

I think Paul Federn gave a few lectures, but I do not

recall what they were about. We were, at that time, too naïve to be listening to Federn's ego psychology, which since then has made quite a bit of noise. He was the real patriarch of the whole movement, because when Freud was absent from society meetings Federn presided. He was the St. Peter of the movement.

I was never impressed with either his great intelligence or his acumen, but almost all the people who were being analyzed in those days in Vienna—that is, the Viennese—were students of Paul Federn. These were Otto Fenichel and Wilhelm Reich, as well as Gustav Bychowski. The latter started with Siegfried Bernfeld, the first analyst to recommend direct observation of the developing child.

The meetings of the Vienna Psychoanalytic Society were the most entertaining, especially that part of the evening devoted to discussion. This is where Freud showed his great mastery over people, and his great mastery over his subject matter. There were several entertaining things that took place at the meetings, one of which consisted of Freud's comments on a paper by Jokel, which had apparently been promised for at least a year or two. Then finally, one day, Freud announced that this much promised paper was to be given in a fortnight. The paper consisted of a statement that chess was an acting out of the Oedipus complex. There were many learned discussions about it from various members of the Society, but when it came to Freud, who always spoke last, he seemed to be quite angered by the proceedings.

He said, briefly, "This is the kind of thinking that

will bring about the downfall of psychoanalysis. If you write a paper stating arbitrarily that chess is a form of acting out of the Oedipus complex, you are saying nothing. Please desist from writing such papers again. It is non-productive and I do not want it." This was a prophetic observation.

Another one of these impressive occasions consisted of a trial which was conducted against Paul Schilder, who had just published a book on hypnosis in which he made no acknowledgments to either Freud's or Ferenczi's ideas. Poor Schilder looked as if he had been dug out of the grave. He looked pale, haggard, defeated, and like a man about to be hanged. But notwithstanding this, I had to admire the courage with which he stood up for his own rights. He was, naturally, immediately attacked for such behavior, as being either psychotic, unanalyzed, or an unconscious plagiarist. The latter was really a kindly version of what had happened; although Federn charitably called it "unconscious" plagiarism, there was nothing unconscious about it. Schilder just did not think that these ideas were worthy of any particular quotation. With regard to being analyzed, Schilder's defense was that there were other people in the room who enjoyed great favor in the Society who had not been analyzed; for example, "Otto Rank, why didn't he take the trouble to be analyzed?" Whereupon the argument became ad hominem. "Why don't you get analyzed?" "Why don't *you* get analyzed?"

In the meanwhile, there was an enormous amount of discussion going on, which lasted about an hour and a half, about what Freud had said here, and what Freud had said there. Apparently, Freud was very little interested in the plagiarism proceedings. But he was apparently both chagrined and amused by the discussions that went on all about him. And the only comment he made that evening had nothing to do with Schilder and his plagiarism, which he apparently dismissed as of no importance.

After the discussion had gone on for about an hour and a half, Freud tapped for order, indicating that he was impatient and wanted these proceedings to end. He said words to the following effect:

"Gentlemen, you treat me with great dishonor. Why do you treat me as if I were already dead? Here you are, sitting among yourselves, discussing what I have said in this paper, what I have said in that paper, and there are quotations to and fro, and I am sitting at the head of the table and nobody so much as asks me, 'What did you really mean?' " He said, "I take this to be an insult, and it worries me, because if this is what you do while I am still among you, I can well imagine what will happen when I am really dead." After this reproach, Freud abruptly adjourned the meeting.

We were all very sorry when these didactic courses were over; we all felt that we had learned a great deal. For the rest of my stay there, I spent part of my days making abstracts of all the important articles which at that time were not available in English. I read those lengthy tracts in German and made notes. Some of the notebooks I still have.

They were very good abstracts. The Schreber case, the autobiography of a paranoiac. It was from this case that Freud drew his conclusions about the nature of paranoia—that is, the person who thinks he is being persecuted unconsciously wants love from his persecutor, represses the idea that he wants this love, and, instead, sees it as hate. Among my other abstracts were Freud's papers on instinct and its vicissitudes, the unconscious, and other such papers. Those were mainly the papers that Freud wrote during the war, when he had plenty of time and very few patients, because it was not until after World War I that they began flocking to him.

Several amusing things happened during the course of analysis in connection with Freud and his contemporaries. One day, I was associating about my college days when the name of William James came up. As a matter of curiosity, I asked Freud whether he had ever met James.

"Oh, yes," he said. He had met him on several occasions, one of which was on his visit to Clark University. "But then," he said, "he came to see me shortly before he died—in 1911, I believe that was," and Freud went into a long description of the greatness of this man. He said this was the only American genius he had ever known. He said, "This was a great man. Furthermore, he had one attribute for which I have unstinted admiration; he spoke German better than I did. That's quite an achievement!"

After this, I said, "Well, Professor, what did he think of you?"

"Oh," said he, "he thought I was crazy." It is this laconic wit and ease with himself that I most remember with feelings of great warmth, even to this day.

5

Vienna—Off the Couch

◆◆◆

W<small>HEN NOT WITH FREUD</small>, I amused myself by attending the music halls, concerts, and, of course, the opera. Once several of my colleagues and I hired a young man, a pianist with the Philharmonic Orchestra, to play for us the entire score of *Der Rosenkavalier*. Also, a very wealthy lady, a patroness of the arts, once invited me to her home to hear a concert version of Strauss's *Der Frau ohne Schatten*.

As for female companionship, it was difficult for the bachelors among us to meet the young women of good families. In Vienna, as in most of Europe, foreigners are not, as a rule, invited to people's homes. So, one day, I had the idea of putting an ad in the local newspaper. I worded it as follows: "Young physician, American, seeking female companionship. I should like to meet with an educated young lady." When I showed this ad to my landlord, Mr. Frankel, he advised me that should I receive any replies, I should not answer them, as there were many stories going around of previous young Americans who had similarly advertised, and who had been lured somewhere and disappeared. So I did not answer any of the letters I received.

However, on New Year's Eve there was a ball, which was sponsored by the city of Vienna every year. I saw a young lady there, asked her to dance, and we seemed to take to each other. After several dances and some light conversation, I persuaded her to remove her mask, and, to my delight, she was quite beautiful. This ball was where the middle-class Viennese families sent their daughters to find husbands. I remained with her all evening, until her mother came to the ball with her younger daughter, to escort her older daughter home if she had not found a suitor. Finding me there, she left, and I had the pleasure of escorting my lovely partner home. Before I left her at the door, I invited her to the opera. She came that once, but she did not go out with me again. I inferred on our last meeting by the things she said that her objection was that I was Jewish. Vienna was notably anti-Semitic even then, so her attitude came as no surprise.

Most of my colleagues and I would gather at the café to wait for our hour with Freud, drinking coffee and gossiping about other students and his colleagues.

One day, I came to Freud feeling rather high and in a euphoric state. After fifteen or twenty minutes, Freud asked me, "What is the matter with you?"

"Nothing," I blithely told him, "is the matter with me."

"Where did you come from?" he asked.

"I was at Oberndorf's home, where I had coffee with him and Monroe Meyer."

The next day, Freud greeted me with, "Now I know what happened to you yesterday. Your friends played a trick on you. They gave you an overdose of caffeine.

You had a caffeine jag—thanks to your fellow students."

The only other time that I came to Freud not my usual self was after a performance the night before of *Tristan und Isolde*. This opera always affects me and leaves me in an emotionally exhausted state. I told Freud, "Don't worry, I'll be all right tomorrow. This is my normal reaction to *Tristan*."

As for my experience with Freud, it was an adventure filled with hypnoidal atmosphere, a charismatic personality of great charm, persuasiveness, and genius, too. I do not know of anyone, inside or outside of this science, who would have had the genius, the passion for observation, the extraordinary ability to deduce the nature of these processes that governed the dream, and which helped make it possible to define the integrative processes that prevail in the formation of the human personality.

As I look back upon this part of my adventure in Vienna, I must make the following comments. First, I was too bewildered by the entire experience, its condensation, its concentration, for it to have given me any kind of perspective whatsoever in the total field. I learned it in about the same way as when I went to parochial school to learn Hebrew. This was a finished dogma, I was learning the TRUTH, and it was eternal, immutable, and there was nothing that would ever change it.

I was puffed up with pride, arrogant as a peacock with having been one of the elect, molded fresh by the hand of the great master himself. However, this did not last long, for I soon discovered that my training was inadequate to the practice of psychoanalysis, and that I had embarked on an odyssey without map or compass.

6

My Analysis as Seen from 1976

FROM MY present vantage point, Freud's analysis was a brilliant performance, done with speed and accuracy. What made Freud such a great analyst was that, at least at that time, he never used theoretical formulations, but made his interpretations in simple language. Except for the use of the concept of the Oedipus complex and unconscious homosexuality, he dealt with the material as it had occurred in life. As an interpreter of dreams, he was brilliantly insightful and intuitive.

Freud immediately recognized that what my condensed dream of the three Italians had uncovered was a situation that belonged to my past. Nature and an alteration of my environment created by my stepmother had built a strong defense in the form of a salutary amnesia. This latter put a protective coating on my unstructured and ego-defeating past. I was afraid—in the form of resistance to the analytic process—of the past, of the past and its recall, and was projecting those fears of what had already happened into a fear of what *would* happen in the future. What I feared to remember and feared to repeat were the feelings of humiliation and helplessness of my early childhood. Freud showed me that these dreams reflected my low self-esteem and the desperate, self-preservative measures which I projected onto convenient danger symbols like my father, Italians, and the like. However, using the dream of intercourse with my stepmother, he also pointed out that these circumstances notwithstanding, I still had a lot of fight in me, and though I might at times be down, I would never be out.

Freud, by identifying and making me aware of those factors around which my fears were clustered, freed me from their inhibitory power and permitted me to come to terms with them. The interpretation of these dreams also finally freed me of my resistance to analysis itself, which I had acquired from Dr. Frink.

Freud's reconstruction of the infantile phobia about masks, and tracking it down to my first encounter with death, was a masterpiece. It was an uncannily intuitive association to the fact, of which I had no conscious memory, that I must have seen my mother dead, if not actually been with her when she died. This also illustrates the mechanism of screen memory. I had no recall at all of being with my mother when she died, or of spending the day in the room with her after her death, and of probably trying to get her attention or some response, to no avail. It was all too painful and frightening an experience, and so I put it all on fearing masks. This fear, though not pleasant, was certainly less painful than remembrance of a mother's immobile, unresponsive face.

But the use made of this extraordinary insight was erroneous. Here he put me on a wild-goose chase for a problem that did not exist. Namely, the use of my identification with my natural mother as a part of an unconscious homosexuality, in order to resolve the Oedipus complex. Freud was convinced that the passive homosexuality constellation was practically universal among all men and remained fixed in the character of the individual, who could do nothing but reconcile himself to it. If one determines sexual adaptation in terms of object of sex drive, then my dream about my stepmother showed that my self-assertive drive toward the woman was totally uninhibited, but everything else we had uncovered showed that my self-assertive drive was, and that was where the problem did lie. The emphasis should have fallen on my unrealistic lack of confidence in myself, my very early picture of the world as a difficult place in which to survive, which augmented my helplessness and increased my dependency on my father. In order to maintain his support, I surrendered my aggressive drive and masked my self-assertion under a cloak of submission.

As a therapeutic tool, this concept of unconscious homosexuality is misleading. It makes the patient address himself to a nonexistent state of affairs and augments his sense of helplessness, thereby confirming his feeling that he cannot direct his own life.

Freud's perspective on the whole problem of development was constricted by his emphasis on unconscious homosexuality and the Oedipus complex. He could have helped me develop self-assertion and, with a little encouragement, this would have been easy because I had a good deal of drive. By making it into a problem of unconscious homosexuality, he turned my attention to a nonexistent problem and away from a very active one.

In his use of the insights of the rag dream (as well as the three Italians), he overlooked the fact that in my relations to him I was doing the same thing I had done with my father. He had sent me into a panic when he informed me of my fear of uncovering a repressed hostility to my father, but failed to point out that this was a pattern that was now operative in the present with Freud and other male authority figures. As with my father, I would repress my self-assertion with Freud in order to maintain his favor and support. The central fact in the transference situation was overlooked by the man who had discovered the very process of transference itself.

Years later, I got into a situation with my peers where this particular adaptive behavior did not work. Then I was really in trouble. I went for a review analysis during my summer vacation in 1931 with Hanns Sachs in Berlin, who merely confirmed the stand that Freud had taken ten years previously. I had to work my way out of it by myself; but I also learned from this self-analysis to discard the hypothesis that put me on such a false trail and to establish a new frame of reference that was free of the blind spot that Freud and his followers put upon the analytic procedure.

One other difference between most analytic methods today and my analysis with Freud is that the process he called *Durcharbeitung* is now an integral part of the analysis itself, the "working through" being done by both the analyst and the patient. Together they bring the insights based on dreams and on the past to bear on the patient's present behavior and functioning.

I would like to add a purely personal note at this
point. I had often thought of my bachelorhood as con-
nected with the previous injuries inflicted on me by my
mother's death, and later by K——'s rejection of me.
Freud, however, did not make much of my unwed state.
He dismissed the matter with a hope that someday I
would be lucky enough to make a good marriage. His
choice of words surprised me. I asked, "Does it require
luck if you know so much about people?" He replied
that it certainly did, because how much can you really
know about anyone until you have lived together, and,
furthermore, it takes many years of living with someone
to really get to know that person. It was not until many
years later, at a time when my zest for life seemed to be
prematurely lagging, that I had the good luck to meet
and marry my wife, and to have a lovely daughter. De-
spite my disastrous early start in life, in the end it turned
out that I was most fortunate in that area where many
people fail, in my close personal relationships.

It is also interesting to observe that my experiences in
an environment that had been unkind to me, and in my
analysis, which revealed how much I had been shaped
by it, stimulated and led me to my particular line of research—first in the studies of environmental stress in the
traumatic neuroses of war, and then in the studies of
different cultures that showed the contingency of culture on character formation of its members.

It took me a long time in practice and the study of
the war neurosis and the characterological end products
of various cultures to recognize that what Freud had
discovered in *The Interpretation of Dreams* was the

anatomy of that process that psychologists had been talking about for a century—the mechanism of the integration of experience toward the end of adaptation. The devices used were condensation, projection, introjection, identification, repression, and the variability of access to awareness (the so-called unconscious); the dominant role of pleasure, un-pleasure, and pain in the formation of these adaptive modalities; and the innumerable ways in which accommodation to existing environmental realities compels the organism to modify these adaptive patterns according to the conditions created by the natural and human environment.

For these reasons alone, if for no other, Freud has earned immortality. He should endure because these are the devices through whose comprehension man can know and direct himself.

7

Return to New York—
The Years After

At the time I returned to New York, in 1922, there were only about ten practicing psychoanalysts in the city, and the New York Psychoanalytic Society, founded by George Kirby, Adolf Meyer, and Macfee Campbell, had been in existence since 1911.

I began to attend its meetings in the year 1919, and I felt highly honored when in February 1920 I received a letter advising that I was elected a member of that organization. The president of the Society was A. A. Brill, who was the original translator of Freud's works, and to whom Freud was therefore heavily indebted for the great reputation that he had in America. Brill had also accompanied Freud on his famous trip to Clark University, where he received the Doctor of Laws degree.

In 1930, in concert with Monroe Meyer and Bert Lewin, I helped found the New York Psychoanalytic Institute, the first psychoanalytic training school in the United States. I remained with that organization until 1941, when, because of theoretical and political differences, I joined Drs. Rado, Levy, and Daniels in a move to Columbia University, where we established the first psychoanalytic training school under the aegis of a university medical school.

However, on my arrival back in the United States, my primary concern was to establish a practice in New York. I opened an office on West Seventy-ninth Street, bought a desk, chair, and the requisite couch, and announced myself "open for business."

My first patient was a man of fifty-seven, married, and the father of two grown sons. He had been a fairly successful businessman and was a pleasant, amiable person. There was one thing wrong, however; he felt he was turning into a goat. He insisted that his body was being covered with goat's hair and his teeth were chattering, goat-fashion, constantly. This was a weird form of depersonalization and a kind of schizophrenia which had no relevancy either to my analysis with Freud or to anything I had learned in Vienna. However, I did my best, using all the orthodox methods which I could think of, and got nowhere. But I had heard of a new therapy method that was fashionable at the time, which was based on the idea that if you placed your patient under stress, he would be more productive. In desperation, I decided to try it on my "goat man." Whatever his other troubles, they had not interfered with his interest in sex and he had therefore remained sexually very active. I decided to put the "stress"—create the pressure, so to speak—here in this area, and therefore forbade him any sexual relations. After about two weeks, his wife called me in great distress. She wanted to know what was happening to her husband. This easygoing, kind man who never before had raised his hand to her or to anyone else was now having outbursts of violent temper, during which he would beat her. This was certainly not the "productivity" I had hoped to produce, and I immediately gave permission for the resumption of sexual activity. Needless to say, the outbursts ceased. Unfortunately, I was eventually obliged to institutionalize him, which was a painful experience for me. Not only had I grown fond of him, but my failure was a severe blow to my self-confidence. My feelings must have been apparent to him, because he kept reassuring me as he was being taken away, "Don't worry, Abie! I'll be all right!"

I had been working at a psychiatric clinic before I left for Vienna, returned there when I first came back to New York, and was almost immediately assigned a patient who presented me with an unusual problem. He was a man about thirty-eight years old, short and heavyset, who looked suspiciously around the room when he was ushered in to see me. He pointed to the secretary and said in a low voice, "Does she have to be in the room?" I replied that I usually kept records, but he asked me to get rid of her, indicating that he did not want anyone else to hear what he had to tell me. I was intrigued, so I dismissed my secretary and asked the man what was on his mind.

He answered, laconically, "I can't do my job any more." Of course I asked him what his job was, and he replied, "I'm a triggerman." Being young and naïve, I didn't know what that meant, and so I asked for a job description. The man explained that he killed people for hire and thus had the highest pay and highest rank in the world of crime. He went on to describe the loss of status and humiliation he'd suffered because he now had to resort to second-story work owing to his inability to pull the trigger—what he called his loss of nerve. Incredulously, I said, "You mean you want me to restore your ability to kill? You want me to take away from you the only decent thing about you, your inability to kill innocent people?" He matter-of-factly said, "Yes." The only thing that seemed to bother him was his doubt about whether or not he should trust me. He wanted to know how he could be sure that the next time he came I wouldn't have the police waiting for him. I, in turn, explained to him about my job, that I was like a priest and could not reveal confidences or confessions. It then occurred to me to ask, "How do I know you won't decide that I know too much?" He grinned and said, "We've got something on each other, ain't we?" Our relationship having been defined to the best of our ability, I told him to give me his life story.

It turned out that by the time he was nine years old both his parents had died. The only place he knew to hang out was the New York docks, where, one day, a tugboat captain invited him to stay on his boat. This meant that my patient could eat regularly and sleep comfortably, so he didn't mind that in return for his security he had to help with the ship's chores and had to be the captain's lover. However, he protested that he was absolutely not homosexual and had no interest in it; to him it had only been a way of making a living. Eventually, he ran away from the captain and sought out some underworld connections he had made around the docks. He started on the lowest rung in the crime hierarchy and worked his way up to being a hit man, although he could never kill without a shot of morphine because it was hard for him to kill without a motive. This fact encouraged me to continue working with him, because, in my naïveté and optimism about my new profession, I felt that this indicated that he had enough decency in him to enable me to cure him of his criminality altogether. However, I only saw the man six or seven times, and then he vanished. I will never know whether I cured him, of either his inability or his ability to kill. I doubt if I did either, or if, given the chance, I would ever try again.

After three months, I left the clinic as well as the job of medical examiner to the Children's Court, which I had also retained from my pre-Vienna days. I had been offered and happily accepted a job at the Veterans Bureau, where I had the opportunity of working with the veterans suffering from shell shock, as the traumatic war neurosis was then called. In these neuroses can be seen paralysis of ego functions like speech, hearing, and sometimes all sense organs. One can also see all stages of regression, some even into infancy. In addition, there can be periodic losses of consciousness, in which traumatic scenes are relived and often re-enacted. There are also instances of paraplegia, hemiplegia, and disturbances of the endocrine and sympathetic nervous systems.

The following case history is a particular favorite of mine, not only because I learned a great deal about regressive states from it, but also because of its oddly humorous ending.

When I first saw T——, he was about thirty years old and, because of his disability, was unable to be steadily employed. All he had to live on was a small government pension. He had been engaged in trench warfare and had been distinguished for exceptional bravery. His trench had been shelled, and he had been buried under earth and debris three times, without any untoward effect. However, after the fourth such occasion, he came to but was mute, deaf, blind, with no body sense, and had to be fed with a dropper. Body feeling returned within six months, and it took another six months for the sensory organs to regain their function. It was more than a year before he could read or write, and it is interesting to note that the latter ability was the last of all to return. When I met him, he had the usual war syndrome of repetitive battle dreams and extreme sensitivity to loud noises, especially unexpected ones, which would often cause him to lose consciousness. This was no epileptic convulsion but a reliving of the last shelling.

I had many sessions with him, in which we talked a great deal and I tried to help him recall and thereby live out the traumatic incident, but it was to no avail. I now feel that this kind of treatment came too late. To be effective, it must be begun in the first three months after the initial injury and certainly not later than six months.

About a year after my attempts at treatment had ended, I invited him to my class at Cornell University. I wanted to demonstrate a "live neurosis" instead of teaching it from a book. He came, I presented him to the class, he was most cooperative, I thanked him, and he left.

When the lecture was over, and I was leaving, I saw him in the lobby. I asked him why he was waiting for me. "Well, Doc, I just wanted to thank you for everything you have done for me."

I replied, quite honestly, "But I never did anything for you. I certainly didn't cure your symptoms."

"But, Doc, you did try. I've been around the Veterans Administration for a long time, and I know they don't even try, and they don't really care. But you did. I just want you to know that if there is anything I can do for you, please let me know."

I thanked him, wished him well, but could not refrain from asking, "Well, T——, what is it you could do for me?"

"Well," he said, cupping the side of his lips with his hand, "if you ever want anyone bumped off, just come to me—I guarantee you I can arrange it."

I have often thought of this most generous offer, and must admit that at certain times over the years I have been been tempted to take T—— up on it.

My efforts to create a theory for the war neuroses proved impossible. Working with the concepts of the libido theory, which are based on instinctual energies, phylogenetically programmed stages of development, and a predetermined Oedipus complex, left little room to explain the response to a traumatic experience, whether in war battle environments or any other situation offering an immediate threat to survival. But I tried and even came up with a sort of innovation. I divided cathexes into bound and mobile, wrote a long paper on the subject, which was published in the *Psychoanalytic Quarterly*, and then abandoned the project.

I did not come back to it until 1939, when, after the publication of *The Individual and His Society*, I was asked to write something on the war neuroses. I looked over my previous work, found it completely unsatisfactory, and realized that I had to reassess the entire theoretical structure. After several attempts, I finally came through with a plausible hypothesis.

The war neuroses showed that defensive and adaptive

maneuvers were very different in character in that sometimes a defensive maneuver can destroy the adaptation of
the entire ego. The key to the syndrome was that in response to a traumatic survival threat from the environment, the defensive shrinkage of the ego destroys the
adaptive capacity of the entire organism. In other words,
the trauma causes the total ego to become disintegrated,
which in turn leads to the breakdown of the ego's systems of action. It is here that one sees the failure of the
adaptive mechanisms such as denial, displacement, and
so on described by Freud in his *Interpretation of Dreams*.
The need to deny, to forget, to not see, is an attempt
to break contacts with, to defend oneself from a dangerous and painful stimulus. But the adaptive maneuver
fails and becomes maladaptive by depriving the individual of some or all of his effective coping devices. Hysterical blindness shuts off the pernicious scene, but unfortunately it blocks out everything else as well.

What I have never been able to understand is that I
was able to come to grips with the war neuroses only
after I had written *The Individual and His Society*,
which concerned itself with the problems of adaptation
in primitive society.

One day in 1932, I suggested to Dr. Sandor Rado, then
director of the New York Psychoanalytic Institute, that
the curriculum should include Freud's sociological writ-
ings. He agreed, and told me to do it. I protested that I
did not know anything about the subject, to which he replied, "Neither does anyone else."

There it was, pure accident, that led to my adventures
in the social sciences. At first, I used the digests of primi-

tive society written by Malinowski and others, brought
to me for seminar study by Cora Du Bois. In 1937, Ralph
Linton brought me his material on the three primitive
societies for which he was the ethnographer, which was
to make up the major part of *The Individual and His
Society*. It was in this seminar in 1938 that I really began
to find myself in new territory and realized the necessity
for certain innovations in psychoanalytic theory. The
libido theory's assumption that most human development
was propelled by certain inborn energies and occurred
under a certain preordained order proved to be unwieldy
and unable to yield the new information in the study of
social processes. What was needed was a method for the
empirical study of ontogenesis, particularly under greatly
varying conditions. The seminars with Linton's material
gave me the opportunity to observe the impact of social
institutions on the human mind and on character formation. I felt I was on the right track, because character
defines the nature of human interaction within a society.
If the interaction is in the main cooperative, then the
society holds together. However, if the social institutions
change too rapidly or create too much tension within individuals, cooperative feelings, which are the glue that
holds any society together, may dissolve and the society
falls apart. Rome is one such example familiar to everyone.

One of Linton's cultures, the Tanala, was most instructive as to the impact of rapid social changes. This
society had lived by means of dry rice cultivation and
had a form of social organization usually found in simple
agricultural societies. It was patriarchal, with the sons

dependent upon the father for food and the father dependent upon the sons for labor. The basic values stressed cooperativeness and obedience. Their myths and religion reflected the lack of violence and combativeness also seen in the society at large. However, because of the disappearance of cultivable land, they had to switch over to wet rice cultivation, which required a different kind of social organization, one that was much more individualistic and competitive. The former social and family relationships had to be broken up, and a new order of each man on his own came into being. The problem was that the needs of the old social organization had created men who tended to be passive, noncompetitive, and with strong controls over their aggression. Now the opposite was needed, and social chaos followed. Those with the greatest amount of drive and aggression pushed forward, and the others fell by the wayside. The social signs of this were a sudden, marked increase in mental breakdowns, crime, homosexuality, and "bad," hostile magic. So here, in a so-called more simple society, we could see the dynamic process of the social distress syndrome that has filled our history books and which we see with us today.

In 1937, Cora Du Bois and I decided that if we really wanted to see the end products of the cultural process, we needed data based on direct observation and a means to detect some of the less visible consequences in the individual. She went to Alor, equipped with tools never before used in ethnography. Not only was she to pay particular attention to the method of child rearing, but she would take personal biographies, dreams, Rorshachs, children's drawings, and the Porteus I.Q. tests for illiterates. She came back from Alor with a masterpiece of ethnography and the most exciting material I had ever encountered. It is this material that formed part of my book *The Psychological Frontiers of Society*, published in 1945.

The chief feature of the Alorese culture was the neglect of the children owing to a division of labor in which the women go to work in the fields at sunrise and return at sundown. The child from shortly after birth is left to the haphazard care of anyone around, including grandparents, siblings, or any passing adult. Maternal neglect is not institutionalized, but the division of labor is, and the neglect of the children has identifiable consequences in the formation of their characters. We then found that their religion, folk tales, and values were consistent with their basic personalities. Their religion was very like the relation of these children to their parents. There was no idealized protective deity but rather one who is called upon only in dire emergencies. They sacrifice reluctantly and do not store up merit. They have no permanent representations of deity or temples; they improvise the effigies for the occasion, then throw them away.

Their folk tales reflect the hatred of the parent as well as their general hostility and lack of feeling for each other. They have a distinctive set of values. They cannot plan in advance, have no consistent life goals, and therefore live from day to day. They tolerate dilapidation and let things go to rack and ruin. They have no artistic sense, and cannot idealize nature, since for them the world has been a constantly traumatic place.

This work on Alor led to some new and exciting in-

115

sights. Among these was the feedback system between a society's institutions and its constituents and the importance for the social effectiveness—and sometimes survival—of creating enough individuals with the emotional capacity for cooperation. And, methodologically, the importance of psychological observation of a culture by direct contact with its individuals as the only way in which we can use psychodynamics to make it yield usable information about the works of society.

Why make personality the central focus of the social process? Because social institutions leave an indelible imprint on the human personality, and knowledge of this impact is exceedingly valuable if one wants to know whether a social pattern is having a good or pernicious effect. There is an ongoing interaction between the human unit and the institutional setup that determines social survival or failure, but since not all the factors in this constant process are visible to the naked eye, the use of this method based on psychodynamics is a most valuable tool. It is therefore possible that the tools brought by psychoanalysis to the social sciences may be one of its important and durable contributions.

8

Fifty-five Years
with Psychoanalysis—
An Appraisal

━━━━━━━━━━━━◄►◄►◄►━━━━━━━━━━━━

THE SUCCESS OF the psychoanalytic movement at this particular time can be seen as the result of certain identifiable factors. A new interest in human character developed because of the important fact that character in industrial society decided one's status opportunities and hence one's fate. This was due to industrialization and democracy as its form of government, which created new opportunities for social and economic mobility, absent in the feudal ethos in which status was determined by birth. As in any caste system, the individual's destiny was out of his hands, while in the new order success or failure became each individual's own responsibility. In view of this, objection to any interference with comfort, happiness, and, especially, effectiveness became a legitimate claim. Psychoanalysis became the standard way of getting a second chance in life, the opportunity for a rebirth with all handicaps removed.

Included in the general clamor for personal success and happiness were claims for more sexual freedom and liberation from the repressive Victorian sexual mores. A most pernicious part of these mores was the absolute belief in the evils of masturbation, on which subject an enormous amount of literature was written. This is of importance because it encouraged parents to forbid masturbation for their children, not only because of church interdiction, but because the secular wisdom of the day saw this practice as leading to all kinds of physical damage. Therefore, parents restrained their children less from moral reasons than from a desire to protect their physical well-being. Insanity, syphilis of the brain, loss of physical energy, and so on were among the medical myths of the day. The method used to control children ranged from all kinds of dire threats to actual physical means, such as the removal of the clitoris in the females. This attitude toward masturbation, and the general puritanical attitude to sex, was responsible for many of the neuroses of the patients that Freud saw. It was largely around this constellation that Freud constructed his libido theory.

Where is psychoanalysis now? From the 1920s through the 1950s, it took hold and flourished, especially in the United States. It held out great hope as a therapeutic tool, and its frame of reference influenced the arts, especially in the area of the theater and literature, while much of it filtered down to the parlance and attitudes of daily life, including education, relations of parents and children, and the relations between the sexes. But since the 1960s, a gradual disillusionment began to set in. Psychoanalysis promised more than it could deliver. Freud himself said that psychoanalysis was good only for *"ein kleine Neurose"*—a small neurosis. But it was turned to as a cure for all kinds of schizophrenias, psychoses, drug addictions, affectlessness, and whatever. In addition, the libido theory and its metapsychology became a closed system which could not be used as a guide to further empirical research.

Unfortunately, for decades all forms of disagreement with any of Freud's ideas were attributed to personal ambition, to a desire to go Freud one better, to resistance, or to just plain orneriness, if not insanity. Attempts at innovation were discouraged by those who had established themselves as Keepers of the Orthodoxy, who had a vested interest in maintaining their power and influence, and could only do so by freezing the field in its existing mold, thereby automatically disqualifying any innovation. As a result, the existing frame of reference was in itself immobilized. For those who are not analysts, this description can only be compared with the experience of indoctrination in a religious dogma. And a science that blocks its own growth tends to resemble a cult. A fresh re-examination of psychoanalysis is imperative for its survival. Otherwise, there is real danger that Freud's great discoveries will be discarded and lost.

Within a single lifetime, he discovered the intra-psychic processes of the human mind which use the unconscious mechanisms of projection, repression, rationalization, and so on. These are the individual's attempts to handle his impulses and motivations, to use controls, and thereby come to some adaptive accommodation with his environment. This adaptive accommodation ends in habitual forms of behavior which are known as character traits.

Freud also discovered the importance of the environment in the development of the human being from infancy to childhood, and he created a method for identifying those experiences which influenced and shaped the kind of adult the child grows up to be. This has impact on parent-child relations, as well as all educational frames of reference. In addition, it helps explain the impact of cultural institutions on the formation of human personality, e.g., What makes a Frenchman different from an Eskimo?

It is my credo that psychoanalysis has only one future and that is as a scientific discipline based on empirical and verifiable observations. We must dedicate ourselves to the following enterprises:

First of all, we must stop studying human beings from the couch. We cannot study human development through retrospective reconstructions. These condensations give too much opportunity for error. We must go into the field and study children directly from birth on.

Secondly, this has to be done not in one culture, but in many cultures, so that we can form some controlled basis for correlations and predictions. Only when this is done can we give the public reliable directives about how to raise children; and it is only from this source that we can gain any reliable ideas concerning prophylaxis, which is the greatest of all the responsibilities of psychoanalysis.

Thirdly, we must study the patterns of social adaptation. I submit to you that there is no social pattern that can function without the closest vigilance. We already know that culture is an extremely vulnerable structure. Its future is not vested in our technology but in the kinds of human beings we cultivate, and in whether the creatures we are creating are capable of cooperative survival.

We must learn to diagnose the ills of our times and what is happening to the human mind in a culture that is changing its basic patterns with explosive rapidity. Then, we have an educational job to do. We shall have to earn public confidence, not by selling hope, but in the same way that physics and chemistry have earned theirs. These two have become honored by man because they increased man's ability to survive. Psychoanalysis has acquired a similar responsibility, and it can become a very essential tool in social as well as human survival.